We Know What You Want
How They Change Your Mind

Martin Howard

disinformation

The Author

Martin Howard has spent over fifteen years in the marketing field with more than ten of them in advertising agencies. He has consulted to a range of organizations in the area of communications and design.

We Know What You Want is Martin Howard's first book. It was inspired by the book *Coercion*, by Douglas Rushkoff.

While witnessing the decline of the traditional advertising agency he became interested in emerging forms of communication and stumbled upon the writings of Marshall McCluhan and others, who charted the profound but underestimated impact of electronic media. Now a strong advocate for media literacy, his interest is in making these theories accessible to average consumers and students.

His aim in this project is to encourage individuals to assess their own media environment and to reclaim their free will.

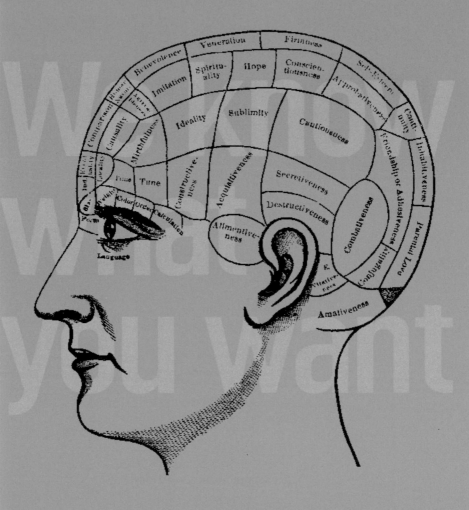

We Know What You Want
How They Change Your Mind

by Martin Howard

CONTENTS

Introduction

These are challenging times for conscious people. More challenging than I usually allow myself to believe.

I originally wrote *Coercion: Why We Listen to What "They" Say* as a primer to the world and ideas I had been describing in my previous books. I had been so excited about the prospect of interactivity, virtual community, and consciousness expansion, that I thought all I needed to do was write about these new possibilities and everyone would jump in. My earliest books, *Cyberia, Media Virus* and *Playing the Future*, were happy announcements of the fact that the tools of reality creation were now in the hands of average people. We could all read the news, report the news, and make the news - as well as anything else we chose to. Seize the day. The world is ours.

I found there were two main audiences for these optimistic forecasts of the effect of new media and new mindsets on our society: counterculture members and marketing executives. The first group consisted mostly of the hackers, computer games, scientists, and culture jammers who already understood most of what I was saying. The other group - who I wasn't really interested in at all - was made up of people working in advertising and public relations. They wanted to know how all these changes would help or hinder their efforts to influence our thoughts and behaviors. They read my books in order to counteract the changes I was celebrating.

The second problem was that although I was able to connect with younger people, who already had some sense of the way that the media (and much of our world) has been constructed to stymie their cognitive capacities, I wasn't able to reach most of their parents. What I realized was that most of America didn't even know that their agency had been compromised in the first place, much less that there was something to do about it. What use had they for the Internet, if they thought the mainstream media was already doing a fine job at telling them the true story, thank you very much?

That's why I took a few steps back, and wrote *Coercion*. Here was my exploration of the people and institutions who mean to control public and private opinions and, more importantly, the techniques they are using. I felt that if I could show the common elements in coercion of all sorts - from advertising to public relations to internet architecture - I would empower people to see these techniques whenever they were being used, and even to challenge them.

Take a simple technique like inducing "regression and transference." All this means is making a person feel small, like a child, and then stepping in as that person's new parent figure. A salesman might do this to a new car buyer, by using technical terms the buyer doesn't understand; a cop might do it to someone he is interrogating; a commercial might do it by intimidating the viewer before introducing the nice gray-haired announcer; the stock market guru might do it right on CNBC. By recognizing the underlying techniques, we stand a much better chance of resisting or, better, defusing them.

The real point of *Coercion* was to show people how influence techniques depend - to some extent - on our participation. The final joke, really, is that *we* are "they," and "they" are powerless without us. We confer respect on our authority figures whether they've earned it or not. We submit to their techniques because we feel ashamed, powerless, at their mercy, or guilty about our own desires. Like any confidence man, the coercer can only exploit a weakness that we refuse to confront directly, ourselves. And that weakness is that while we complain about the way others coerce us, very often - whether at work or church - it is we who are using those very same techniques to coerce someone else.

Coercion met with a lot of acclaim - especially from people outside the marketing world. Emails came in from teachers, senators, artists, and consumer advocates. They all wanted to use the text - or some part of it - in their education programs, anthologies, documentaries or white papers. And pretty much everyone wanted me to create a companion manual to the book - a visual, practical guide to identifying psychological manipulation in our world, and learning to break its hold over us.

Luckily for my own already overbooked life, a brilliant and energetic writer named Martin Howard pinged me about five years ago to ask if I was planning to write a *Coercion* companion - some kind of workbook that pulled out the most useable ideas from the text and made them even more accessible to and actionable by the modern reader. This way, even a non-reader (and that's most of us, these days) would be able to get the gist of these ideas - and even those who do read would get a more user-friendly presentation of this material, complete with some new case studies and high-impact, easily remembered visuals.

Of course I was all for it, and the result of Martin's work - the quintessence of *Coercion* - is in your hands.

But let me also, dear reader, give you a quick disclaimer. I began the book *Coercion* with an extended introduction that demonstrated a bunch of different rhetorical techniques. I wanted to show from the outset that books, too, are influential in their own way. We can't help but use influence techniques, to some extent, whenever we communicate with one another. We wouldn't be speaking if we didn't want to make some change in the other person.

The format of this book is alive with visuals and packed with persuasive language. And while it's sometimes fun to descend into the conspiratorial mindset for a moment, please realize that there's a bit of a wink-wink-nudge-nudge to all of this. Yes, there are nasty people out there in government and corporations who mean to compromise your ability to think. That's just a fact. But this doesn't mean that these people comprise a great and all-powerful "they" who can make you do anything they want to.

It's fun and useful to identify the enemy, see his techniques, and then disable them. It's not useful, however, to become so obsessed with the "theys" out there that we lose sight of our own participation in the game. There is no they without us, and the more we glamorize and obsess on their techniques, the less able we feel to get beyond them.

So please enjoy the style and tone of this volume for what it is: a way to make some of the scariest things about our propagandistic landscape have a bit less hold over us. It's a kind of ghost story, really. Yes, it's scary - so is the idea of a "they" - but the enemies here are just spirits, and only as real as we allow them to be.

--Douglas Rushkoff

New York City, 2004

The Retail Zone

"About 80 percent of consumer choices are made in store and 60 percent of those are impulse purchases."

Herb Meyers, CEO Gerstman + Meyers, New York

We Know What You Want
Chapter 1: **The Retail Zone**

The retail sector has burst beyond the quaint confines of the corner shop. Now it's a multi-sensory market interface for banks, health care professionals, oil companies and religious cults – and their predatory tactics are fine tuned for the street-smart as well as the young and vulnerable. Reclaim your free will and alert yourself to the new agenda with these case studies and insider tips.

In this chapter:

- **Who controls the sale?**
- **Is your doctor really objective?**
- **How to avoid credit traps**
- **Subliminal programming**
- **Showroom mindgames**
- **Muzak mysteries**

MIND CHANGER

Don't look UP!
You might save 50%

PLANOGRAMS: Guiding your eyes to *their* choice

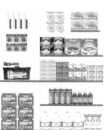

The plans for arranging products on shelves to shift attention to specific products are call planograms. Quantity and positioning are tweaked using computer programs and buyer patterns. Some companies pay a "slotting allowance" for optimum placement.

Expensive breakfast cereals, toys and sweets are often placed at children's eye level. Pester power is worth billions to big brands.

MIND CHANGER ◎

Toy marketers use kids to target parents' wallets

Marketers are hiring child psychologists to get inside young minds in order to develop new toys and advertising techniques. The methods being used are so unethical that a group of American psychologists have protested. Ads designed to coax kids into nagging their parents to buy are now under scrutiny. If your child has just spent Saturday morning watching cartoons, don't be surprised if your shopping outing is hijacked by a tantrum at the toy shop. *More about this problem in Chapter 4 - The Personal Zone*

CLOSE-UP

Supermarkets, Showrooms and Malls

Supermarkets are scientifically designed to guide your every impulse. Eye-level metrics, changing floor layouts and an overwhelming volume of products baffle the unwary shopper in every major store. If you come out of the shop with more than what was on your shopping list – that was the plan.

This principle is also extended to the shopping mall. Take a look around at the people drifting past you with glazed eyes and a robotic walking style. That's the perfect state for a customer to be in.

Showroom tactics focus more on hand-to-hand methods of persuasion. The aim is to get a decision out of you before you're really ready, and, when you're at the counter, to UP-SELL! If you can't afford it, that's okay; they make money when they extend you credit.

TACTIC: Revolving supermarket layouts

If you've ever spent half an hour looking for three products at a supermarket, don't blame yourself. That's just the scientifically-designed store plan doing its job. Supermarkets are designed more to distract you than to assist you. Sauces may be in three different aisles. Cordial is never near the soft drinks, and those big mountains of impulse items at the end of each aisle will catch your attention every time. Just when you think you are finding your way around the store, managers will change the layout. Some stores actually switch the layout every six months to intentionally confuse shoppers.

RESOURCE: The dark side of your supermarket

This downloadable e-book takes you on a trip to the dark side of your local supermarket. It features a deconstruction of the manipulating influences of music and visuals, through to product placement techniques and package design. There is an extensive examination of the environmental and economic impact of store products, as well as insight into additives and genetic modification. Find out how to conduct your own live tour of a local supermarket and turn it into a learning experience.

pirg.uwaterloo.ca/download/docs/TheSupermarketTour.pdf

FACT: Kids influence big spending

Toys are never advertised to parents. Marketing budgets are poured into focus groups and research to find out how to trap little minds. But the target is your wallet. Kids influence up to $500 billion a year in purchases. You might carefully prepare your shopping list, but along the way you'll spend extra on ice-cream, toys and confectionery that your kids demand. It's called Pester Power, and ad gurus are using it as their latest tool to get under your radar.

INSIDER SECRET: The Gruen Transfer

Named after Victor Gruen, the man who invented the first shopping mall in 1956, the Gruen Transfer is the term used by insiders to describe the moment when a shopper enters a daze and loses full control of the decision-making process. Symptoms include glazed eyes, loss of direction and suggestibility. It is in this pliable mental state that you are most likely to make an unplanned purchase – the condition that store managers prefer all customers to be in BEFORE entering their store.

FACT: Branded fruit

Our fruit is now an advertising space ripe for the plucking, thanks to the efforts of Irv Weinhaus, president of Fruit Label Co., who arranged a deal with Universal

"We want you to get lost." Tim Magill- Designer, Mall of America

Malls and shopping centers are mazes designed to keep you disorientated, with odd-shaped floor layouts, special music and café aromas.

The point at which you lose full consciousness of your decisions is known as the Gruen Transfer.

Today's supermarkets carry over 30,000 different products in each store. They make more money when you ignore your shopping list, so they play muzak tracks that will program you to stay longer.

"Department-store customers exposed to Muzak shop 18% longer and make 17% more purchases. Grocery shoppers respond best to Muzak that has a slower tempo, making a whopping 38% more purchases when it is employed. Fast-food restaurants use Muzak that has a higher number of beats per minute to increase the rate at which patrons chew their food." - Coercion

POWER TUNES

muzak

"We create experiences with audio architecture. Our art is to capture the emotional power of music and put it to work for your business. Crafted by a talented group of audio architects, our music programs are designed to create experiences that are both powerful and persuasive.

"One thing we've learned over the past seven decades is that music in all of its incarnations is wondrous and wild. When harnessed properly it can be an extraordinarily persuasive tool. But don't just take our word for it, take a listen instead."

www.muzak.com

MIND CHANGER

The Pulling Power of AROMA

Sensory membranes in your nose are directly connected to your brain, and process input without the same filters as your other senses. This is why particular smells can evoke strong memories, bring on illness or feelings of euphoria.

Publicity material for aroma marketing company Ecomist assures retailers that their scent-dispensing machines will induce "appropriate moods" in customers.

"Ensure that your business smells great and enhance your sales and customer retention... The Ecomist Aroma Marketing system employs the latest dispensing technology and a selection of over 50 fragrances to put the appropriate aroma in your service or retail environment ... essential oils will effect appropriate moods in your clients making the experience with you more pleasant and memorable."

www.ecomist.co.nz

TAKE CONTROL Switch your senses back on! Stay in touch with your moods and make a note of changes.

The Scented Shopping Mall Experiment

One olfactory marketing specialist proved the commercial value of smell with an experiment in a Montreal-area shopping centre. Jean-Charles Chebat, from the University of Montreal's HEC management school, pumped discreet traces of a sweet citrus fragrance (a combination of lemon, orange, grapefruit and tangerine) into the mall's air for a week. "The shoppers didn't even know the scent was there because the airborne dose was so tiny," Chebat explains. Merchants, however, certainly smelled a difference: purchases that week were up by $55 to $90 per customer, even though the experiment was conducted during a traditionally slow business period and the stores had been instructed to offer no special sales or promotions.

www.enroutemag.com/english/february03/scent_eng1.htm

Home Studios to promote Jim Carrey's *Liar, Liar* on 12 million apples.

Fruit Label is making millions in revenue each year, including a half-million dollar deal to advertise a dot-com on 175 million bananas, apples and oranges.

www.thefruitlabelco.com

TACTIC: Bait and switch

When you spy a great bargain in the discount electrical catalog, it might be step one in the bait-and-switch technique. Sometimes it's a massively discounted television set or refrigerator. If you turn up at the store ready to buy, you might find the item out of stock, or find a clever saleman who shows you an item that's "even better." Since you're excited about the item and may have made up your mind to purchase it, it's now that much easier for you to be steered into another sale. If you've entered the store with the intention to purchase, you will find it very hard to leave without thinking that you've wasted time. The salesman knows that most people are impatient in this situation, and will use this to upsell you to an item of HIS choice.

TACTIC: Showroom manipulation

When you walk into a car showroom, you are in the salesman's territory. Who is controlling the sale? If it isn't you, then you won't be making the decisions. Do you have a clear purpose? If you're not prepared, you may drive out owning an expensive vehicle that you can't afford. Carefully planned sales and financing ploys can keep the deal moving faster than you can handle. The key is control.

Signs that you are being manipulated:

1. They walk away and leave you waiting for 10-15 minutes;
2. They start pushing you into an extended warranty;
3. They swap salesmen;
4. They make a mistake adding up your price;
5. They play mind games during the test drive;
6. They say "this is the last one";
7. They pressure you to "buy today."

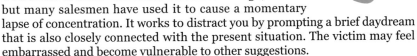

TACTIC: Disassociation

Some salesmen use a special psychological technique called "disassociation" during the test drive, which can make you vulnerable. They will ask "Is this the type of vehicle you would like to own?" It sounds harmless enough, but many salesmen have used it to cause a momentary lapse of concentration. It works to distract you by prompting a brief daydream that is also closely connected with the present situation. The victim may feel embarrassed and become vulnerable to other suggestions.

TACTIC: Follow the script, please!

"When you walk into a GAP store, a young clerk will initiate a well-researched sales technique called GAPACT (Greet Approach Provide Add-on Close Thank). Should we be mad at her? Of course not. She's just doing what her manager has told her to do. If she doesn't end the day with a certain quota of multiple-item sales, she'll get in trouble. So do we blame her manager? No. He's got to meet a quota, too, set by corporate headquarters. Do we blame the marketing department? Well, they're just taking their orders from the CEO. And he's just taking his from the Board of Directors. And they're just listening to their shareholders. And those shareholders, well, they're some of the same people walking in the door as customers, who happen to have GAP stock in the mutual funds of their retirement plans." - *Coercion*

> **DEFINITION**
> ### *disassocia-tion*
> A psychological defense mechanism in which specific, anxiety provoking thoughts, emotions or physical sensations are separated from the rest of the psyche.

FACT: Subliminal encoders

A firm that builds sound "encoders" claims that subliminal programming is one of the most misunderstood and underrated performance-enhancing tools of the decade. "Subliminal programming is the act of conveying a message below the threshold of conscious awareness. Lorelei Communication Group can supply your retailer with a machine costing up to $3000 that will encode the message of your choice and play it to your customers."

The manufacturer's website boasts "the most advanced form of mind control available."

www.lorelei.com

TREND: Loyalty cards invade your personal privacy

While customer loyalty cards have become an attractive inducement for people wanting to save some money, they also reduce your privacy. Databases that connect to these cards track every purchase you make over a period of years, and connect it to all the demographic data that you supplied in your initial application. Consumer advocates also claim that stores use purchasing data for "redlining," a practice where big discounts are offered in neighborhoods whose residents are least likely to take advantage of them. Others warn that personal data can be handed over to government agencies.

TAKE !
CONTROL
Make your purchasing decisions before you enter the shop. Ask the manager about its policy on music.

The emerging use of RFID tags on products is adding even greater surveillance capability, enabling stores to monitor the location of every product sold – in real time. Read more about RFID tags in Chapter 5.

nocards.org, privacyinternational.org

CASE STUDY: Loyalty data tracks obesity

A New Hampshire research group devised a way to use loyalty card data to track family eating habits. Claiming the health benefits of the system, the organization (Yale-Griffin Prevention Center) planned to use datamining to identify families who showed a history of buying certain high-calorie products, and then send them discount offers on healthy products. Although the system has not yet been implemented, British MPs including David Hinchcliffe suggested that a similar strategy be used to stem Britain's obesity crisis. Read more about datamining tags in Chapter 5. *BBC News, Dec 4, 2003*

CLOSE-UP
Financial Institutions

Deregulation of financial institutions has triggered an outbreak of aggressive predatory lending. The victims are disadvantaged low-income families and shoppers who have run out of money. They are enticed by high-pressure salesmen who offer them high interest finance to close the sale.

TREND: Can't afford it? That's okay, we'll sell you the money too!

Apart from increasing their primary business of selling you a life-long debt, banks have spread their influence to the point of sale. To ensure that no customer can use the excuse of not having enough money, financial products enable salesmen to clinch deals with high interest loans and easy payment schemes. These loans generally come with inflated interest rates. Special store cards are bank financial tools to seduce the impulse buyer into quick decisions.

Paying for "easy money"

Predatory loans, credit cards, payday loans, home equity loans, credit lines. In 2003, American consumers owed about $1.7 trillion in credit card and other debts – an amount roughly equal to the gross national product of England and Russia combined.

Banks fall over themselves to give you money. It's tempting. Yet over one million Americans will go into bankruptcy this year. Promises of extra cash for general spending play on consumer greed without mentioning the cost.

Consumers are under constant pressure to buy more. Banks and other lenders come to the rescue with immediate cash. Law suits have been taken out against some banks that have deliberately targeted low income consumers with false promises of rebuilding their finances.

- Remember, banks prey on people's greed.

- Don't look to a personal loan to resolve financial problems.

- Loans are easy to get. Calculate the long-term price.

- Don't make decisions about finance when you are under emotional stress.

REPORT: Credit card deception

Deceptive credit card offers and practices are sinking more and more consumers into high-cost credit card debt, according to a survey of 100 credit card offers released by the U.S. Public Interest Research Group (U.S. PIRG). To fight the practices the report identifies, U.S. PIRG also announced a new credit card education campaign describing how consumers can avoid credit card hazards.

"Credit card companies aren't satisfied with a fair profit, so they're gouging consumers with outrageous interest rates as high as 30% APR," says Ed Mierzwinski, Consumer Program Director for U.S. PIRG. "Credit card marketing has become reckless and deceptive, and sometimes violates consumer protection laws. These deceptive tactics are used by some of the country's largest card issuers and affect millions of consumers each year."

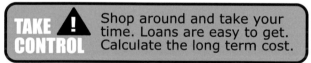

TAKE ⚠ CONTROL Shop around and take your time. Loans are easy to get. Calculate the long term cost.

www.truthaboutcredit.org/release.html

CLOSE-UP
Medical Professionals

Pharmaceuticals are a multi-billion dollar industry. Doctors are the pawns used to push expensive treatments using their privileged aura of unquestionable ethics and bond of trust. If your doctor is taking cash handouts from the company who manufactures your new prescription pills, his first priority may not be your good health.

TREND: Doctors under pressure

"When you ask your doctor about medication, you trust him with your body. You allow the doctor to make the decision, expecting the highest level of judgment and professional ethics when your health is in the balance. For some doctors there are other factors to consider.

"A depression treatment called Celexa was pitched to doctors at a luxurious resort. After a free breakfast, the doctors participated in a morning discussion about depression, which can be treated with Forest's best-selling product, Celexa. Following free lunch, each doctor was handed $500.

"A study published in 2000 in the AMA's journal concluded that doctors who have regular interactions with drug companies are influenced in their prescribing behavior by the gifts and perks they accept.

"Drug companies use these getaways to place doctors on an "advisory committee" which allows them to compensate the doctors directly, without being hampered by AMA guidelines – which are designed to prevent unethical relationships between doctors and drug companies."

–The Wall Street Journal

Patients in South Florida being treated for depression received unsolicited free samples of

PROZAC

in the mail.

A study published in 2000 in the AMA's journal concluded that doctors who have regular interactions with drug companies are influenced in their prescribing behavior by the gifts and perks they accept.

$$$$

Just take these.

INSIDER SECRETS: Drug promotion

An organization which tracks unethical medical practices highlights these key problem areas:

- Drug companies spend an average of 35% of sales on promotion.

- Companies would not spend such massive amounts on promotion if it were not effective at influencing prescribing.

- Promotion influences prescribing much more than most health professionals realize.

- Many advertisements and statements from pharmaceutical representatives are misleading.

- Promotion that exaggerates benefits and glosses over risks threatens optimal treatment.

- Reliance on promotional information may endanger lives and expose prescribers to the risk of litigation.

www.healthyskepticism.org/problem.htm

FACT: Free drugs lure the vulnerable

Illegal drug dealers are notorious for offering freebies to get users hooked on heroin or crack cocaine. In early 2002, around 300 patients in South Florida being treated for depression received unsolicited free samples of Prozac in the mail. One of these patients sued her doctor, her pharmacy and Eli Lilly, Prozac's manufacturer, for invasion of privacy. Lilly issued an apology and conducted an internal investigation.

Promomagazine.com, Vaccinationnews.com

INSIDER TACTIC: Invented syndromes

One drug company started a massive public relations campaign to build awareness of a new disorder for which they had just developed a remedy. In 1998, news bulletins and talk shows started mentioning a new syndrome known as "Social Anxiety Disorder," or SAD. The intention was to build publicity for an illness that nobody knew they yet had, and then come out with the miracle cure – Paxil, an anti-depressant. The scheme worked – producing 50 press stories, websites, professional endorsements and quizzes with names like "Do you have social anxiety disorder?" Symptoms – which included blushing, sweating, trembling and speech difficulties – sounded very much like nervousness or shyness. The campaign, which had been devised by PR consultancy firm Cohn & Wolfe and financed by GlaxoSmithKline, generated massive sales for Paxil.

Paxil.com

CIA spy techniques live on in modern boutiques and sales programs

The Kubark Manual

"By elevating the coercive process to a philosophy of life, books like Carnegie's legitimize people-handling. It's a set of techniques so well proven that the U.S. Central Intelligence Agency includes it in its interrogation manual. The CIA's Kubark manual, written in 1963, was designed to help their operatives elicit confessions and intelligence from detainees. There are no references to rubber hoses or electric shocks. Apparently the mind games of salesmen like Spivas work better than overt torture.

"The CIA structures its noncoercive interrogations in four main parts, loosely corresponding to each section of Dale Carnegie's book... The influence techniques promoted by Dale Carnegie and refined by the CIA have been adapted and upgraded by a wide variety of industries..."

CLOSE-UP

How to Win Friends and Influence People

NOW OVER 7,432,000 COPIES SOLD

HOW TO WIN FRIENDS AND INFLUENCE PEOPLE BY DALE CARNEGIE

1. What are the six ways of making people like you? See pages 57-198.
2. What are the twelve ways of winning people to your way of thinking? See pages 196-170.
3. What are the nine ways to change people without giving offense or arousing resentment? See pages 173-199.

Dale Carnegie's book *How to Win Friends and Influence People* (1936) has sold more than 10 million copies, and has been translated into many languages. His books legitimized the concept of personal manipulation for social development and wealth building. The book has been revered by salesmen and success seekers for decades.

CIA

"...to induce disorientation, regression, transference and compliance... Specialists in larger businesses like retailing, marketing and, perhaps most of all, automotive sales have learned to systematize the tools of the hand-to-hand coercer for more effective use. Today, car salesmen work from prepared scripts that are revised and improved based on our increasing resistance to their methodology. It amounts to a tactical war between America and its automotive industry.

"While traveling salesmen and government operatives depend on their own limited experiences and the insights of psychologists, car dealers are the beneficiaries of corporate-sponsored research. It's a big business, one that dwarfs mechanical bed salesmen and counterespionage agents alike. The millions of us who have been through the car-buying process serve as the massive experimental sample on which the system is refined. If too many of us learn to resist a particular technique, that method is reworked and then camouflaged into a new one.

"Car salesmen are indoctrinated to their dealership's selling systems through video and audio cassettes, customized literature and live seminars."

- Coercion

"Hypnosis offers one advantage not inherent in other interrogation techniques or aids: the post-hypnotic suggestion. Under favorable circumstances it should be possible to administer a silent drug to a resistant source, persuade him as the drug takes effect that he is slipping into a hypnotic trance, place him under actual hypnosis as consciousness is returning, shift his frame of reference so that his reasons for resistance become reasons for cooperating, interrogate him, and conclude the session by implanting the suggestion that when he emerges from trance he will not remember anything about what has happened."

C.I.A.
KUBARK
Counterintelligence Interrogation
M A N U A L

Kubark Interrogation Manual - CIA 1963

"All coercive techniques are designed to induce regression. As Hinkle notes in 'The Physiological State of the Interrogation Subject as it Affects Brain Function,' the result of external pressures of sufficient intensity is the loss of those defenses most recently acquired by civilized man: '...the capacity to carry out the highest creative activities, to meet new, challenging, and complex situations, to deal with trying interpersonal relations, and to cope with repeated frustrations. Relatively small degrees of homeostatic derangement, fatigue, pain, sleep loss, or anxiety may impair these functions.' As a result, 'most people who are exposed to coercive procedures will talk and usually reveal some information that they might not have revealed otherwise.'

"One subjective reaction often evoked by coercion is a feeling of guilt. Meltzer observes, 'In some lengthy interrogations, the interrogator may, by virtue of his role as the sole supplier of satisfaction and punishment, assume the stature and importance of a parental figure in the prisoner's feeling and thinking. Although there may be intense hatred for the interrogator, it is not unusual for warm feelings also to develop. This ambivalence is the basis for guilt reactions, and if the interrogator nourishes these feelings, the guilt may be strong enough to influence the prisoner's behavior.... Guilt makes compliance more likely....'"

Kubark Interrogation Manual - CIA 1963

The Event Zone

"Personal characteristics vanish in the crowd, which exerts an extraordinary influence upon the individuals which form it. The miser becomes generous, the skeptic a believer, the honest man a criminal, the coward a hero."

GUSTAVE LE BON, French Sociologist, 1895

We Know What You Want
Chapter 2: **The Event Zone**

There's nothing like the excitement of a crowd. Whether it is the frenzy of a football final, the worship of a rock legend or the inspirational highs of a motivational seminar, they are powerful and memorable events. The electric atmosphere plays on sentiments and sensations that are common to all of us. Cults, corporations and political parties exploit the crowd dynamics at public events to position their product. It wasn't long before politicians and corporations spotted the opportunity to manipulate the situations for power and profit.

Psychologists have studied how individuals tend to lose control in large groups due to the unique dynamics of crowds – the wide-eyed excitement of the masses opens the way for mind manipulation.

- Rock concerts
- Crowd influence techniques
- Motivational seminars
- Mass meetings
- Stadiums and sport

CLOSE-UP

Music Concerts

Live music crowds can be frenzied or delirious, and with the addition of legal and illegal drugs, fans can become easy prey for merchandisers and dazzling billboards. The show puts the brain in a state that corresponds to the advertisers' requirements – excited, carefree, impulsive and impressionable.

Merchandise malls capture the mobs swarming around the big event, and big companies gamble that some of your happy memories of the event will rub off on their logo. The artistic connection between performer and the audience is merely a vehicle for a series of much larger transactions.

TREND: Mesmerized audiences sold in bulk

"Adoring fans become lost in the excitement of seeing their music idols, and companies have found that their altered state opens up a shortcut to their wallets.

"With 25,000 events in 1998, Robert Sillerman of SFX concert promotions delivered 58 million demographically desirable consumers to advertisers. Sillerman is emphatic about the pliability of this captive audience: 'These are people voting with their feet and their wallets,' says Sillerman. 'If you go see Tom Petty or the Spice Girls, you've chosen to do it. You're excited. You're not doing this passively – like watching TV at home. You're spending money, and you're very receptive to hear direct or subliminal messages.' Indeed, SFX's ads in trade magazines aimed at advertisers read, 'Remember that magical moment when your daughter's eyes widened to meet her favorite characters live on stage? . . . It's exciting, it's magical, it's completely engrossing. And we found a way to package it.'"

– *New York Magazine*, *November 15, 1999*

FACT: Perfect consumers come in crowds

You might think that you have chosen your favorite drink independently, but how can you know for sure? All kinds of decisions are made by your subconcious as a result of subtle pressure. When psychologist Gustave Le Bon discussed the attributes of individuals in crowds he was also describing the ideal, compliant, unquestioning consumer:

"Man, as part of a multitude, is a very different being from the same man as an isolated individual. His conscious individuality vanishes in the unconscious personality of the crowd... Among the other characteristics of crowds, we must note their infinite credulity and exaggerated sensibility, their short-sightedness, and their incapacity to respond to the influences of reason. Affirmation, contagion, repetition and prestige constitute almost the only means of persuading them. Reality and experience have no effect upon them. The multitude will admit anything; nothing is impossible in the eyes of the crowd."

TAKE ⚠ CONTROL

Are you paying more for your tickets each year? If your favourite band is carrying ads or sponsorship, your tickets should be getting cheaper, right? If not, speak up!

Companies have realized this, and concert organizers know that fans and performers won't object to cool-looking ads decorating the stadium.

CASE STUDY: Hip-hop acts promote brands to get by

Sports apparel brands Pony and Puma turned to sponsorship deals to help resurrect their names. Metal band Korn, which previously sported Adidas, and even had a song called "A.D.I.D.A.S.," switched to Puma more than three years ago when Puma offered to give the band free clothes and feature them in a Super Bowl commercial. Korn accepted and began to wear Puma products as opposed to Adidas. Their impulsive action to change styles left fans in the dark. Fans bought Adidas so they could show respect and represent Korn. Now fans don't know whether to change to Puma or to stop wearing them altogether.

"Man, as part of a multitude, is a very different being from the same man as an isolated individual. His conscious individuality vanishes in the unconscious personality of the crowd...

Among the other characteristics of crowds, we must note their infinite credulity and exaggerated sensibility, their short-sightedness, and their incapacity to respond to the influences of reason. Affirmation, contagion, repetition and prestige constitute almost the only means of persuading them. Reality and experience have no effect upon them. The multitude will admit anything; nothing is impossible in the eyes of the crowd."

GUSTAVE LE BON

"If you go see Tom Petty or the Spice Girls, you've chosen to do it. You're excited. You're not doing this passively – like watching TV at home. You're spending money, and you're very receptive to hear direct or subliminal messages."

Robert Sillerman, SFX Concert Mogul (Sillerman sold SFX to Clear Channel in 2000, for $4.4 billion)

TREND: Concert organizers sell your spare attention

Your hundred dollar ticket isn't enough to buy an ad-free performance anymore. With a monopoly over thousands of major music events each year, Clear Channel is big enough to control the number of commercial messages that are included with each concert – and prices for parking, merchandise and beverages are being bumped up. The sponsored performance is now tied in to simultaneous radio commercials to get you from every angle.

"Each of us feels that there is a single 'I' in control. But that is an illusion that the brain works hard to produce – the brain does have supervisory systems in the prefrontal lobes and anterior cingulated cortex, which can push the buttons of behavior and override habits and urges. But those systems are gadgets with specific quirks and limitations: they are not implementations of the rational free agent traditionally identified with the soul or the self."

"Self as a necessary illusion," Halligan & Oakley, 2000

TAKE ⚠ CONTROL

Keep to a budget for post concert fan merchandise. Your post concert impulse purchases are triggered by someone else to make *them* richer. Set yourself a limit and leave your credit card at home

FACT: Instant merchandise malls trap fans...

as fans hunt for merchandise after the show. Some are expanding and turning into marketing malls. The trade show atmosphere includes wine-tasting tents, product sampling and other promoters who pay for the rights for their patch of turf outside.

INSIDER TACTIC: Post-concert ambush marketing

The post concert daze makes you easy prey for merchandise peddlers. Whether you're high on life or something harder, you're much more likely to dive for your credit card. The experts call it ambush marketing:

"Getting the ambush marketing message seen can be done boldly or via a surprise attack. For example, using models clad in bikinis with a company's logo painted on their bodies is a relatively bold way to attract onlookers, while a surprise attack would use an individual or group or people positioned in the crowd to hold up a sign bearing the company logo just as the camera is focused on them."

www.onpoint-marketing.com

TREND: Renaming stadiums with brands

When the DJ or talk show host mentions the latest sellout concert, chances are that they will mention the name of the venue. Brand managers have picked up on this, and are lining up to secure "naming rights" for every major venue.

The opportunity to brand a major landmark means companies like FedEx or Philips can sneak their name into millions of conversations both private and public.

Naming rights are a bargain for big companies. Both in the price tag of the naming rights and in the total "impressions" the naming rights sponsor achieves.

FEDEX paid $205 million to call the Washington Redskins' home "FedEx Field."

So where did you go to see Britney®

Oh she totally rocked **FedEx**® Field!

CLOSE-UP

Motivational Seminars

Training seminars are a fixture of modern business. Sales motivation "congresses" and other seminars are used to build communication skills and success techniques. Some of these fall into a category known as Large Group Awareness Training (LGAT) using a methodology which some label that of a white-collar cult. Fortune 500 companies and individuals shell out millions each year to motivational gurus who use a tested five day formula to guide them to higher performance and personal power. While some attendees become lifelong disciples for the method, others object to the highly confrontational and disturbing tactics that they are asked to endure. Highly experienced facilitators use crowd dynamics as social proof that the "life changing" tactics are valid, but some delegates have found themselves needing psychiatric care by the fourth day.

Large Group Awareness Training programs

Large Group Awareness Training (LGAT) programs are a category of training seminars that use a four or five day formula which promises radical personality change. Attendees are attracted by the prospect of reaching their full potential, or higher success in their career, or in personal relationships. The programs use a three stage process to enable personal growth.

1. Psychological breakdown and opening the subconcious

2. Releasing of repressed emotions, especially those from childhood

3. Rebirthing or rebuilding of personal attitudes

Although many attendees succeed in achieving personal breakthroughs and career success, others are disorientated by the confrontational techniques.

"Large Group Awareness Training (LGAT) programs are personal development training programs in which dozens to hundreds of people are given several hours to several days of intense instruction aimed at helping participants begin to discover what is hindering them from achieving their full potential and living more satisfied lives. LGAT programs have also been developed for corporations and public agencies, where the focus is on improving management skills, conflict resolution, general institutional strengthening, and dealing with the eternal problem of employees who drink too much or use too many drugs. Ultimately, the main product being sold by human potential gurus is hope itself."

– *The Skeptic's Dictionary, www.skepdic.com*

Problems with some powerful training programs

"...most of the nationally known LGATs and a burgeoning, but as yet undetermined number, of take-offs on them are using powerful psychological techniques capable of stripping individuals of their psychological defenses, inducing behavioral regression, and promoting regressive modes of reasoning. Further, it appears that deceptive sales techniques are involved in promoting the trainings since the secrecy surrounding the programs' sales promotions prevents consumers from obtaining full disclosure. Consumers are persuaded to purchase programs described as educational, while in actuality the programs consist of highly orchestrated, intense indoctrination processes capable of inducing marked psychological experience. Consumers are not fully and adequately informed about the programs' intensity, the new philosophical formulations of reality that they imply, the potentially harmful consequences of some of the exercises to which participants will be exposed, the sometimes lurid psychological upset they will witness, nor the fact that management is aware of at least some of the risks to which they subject participants. Such practices run counter to American Psychological Association recommendations on the running of growth groups (American Psychological Association, 1973)."

Report of the APA Task Force on Deceptive and Indirect Techniques of Persuasion and Control November 1986

TAKE CONTROL

Do your own research to familiarize yourself with suspect seminar companies. Factnet.org keeps track of groups that use questionable tactics.

GET
POWER
SUCCESS
LOVE
NOW!

How to spot a dangerous personal development program

Quick Test

Here are some tell-tale signs that a group could be crossing the line and using harmful coercive techniques

- ☐ Secrecy around the processes and techniques used.
- ☐ Programs built on the ideas of one charismatic person.
- ☐ Nagging doubts about the facilitators, staff or program content.
- ☐ Defensive responses to your questions.
- ☐ Vague or over-general promises of participant success.
- ☐ "Hard-sell" tactics.
- ☐ Pressure on graduates to recruit more participants.
- ☐ Refusal to talk to or coordinate with your therapist or counselor.

Mind Blowing!

"The programs consist of highly orchestrated, intense indoctrination processes capable of inducing marked psychological experience. Consumers are not fully and adequately informed about the programs' intensity, the new philosophical formulations of reality that they imply, the potentially harmful consequences of some of the exercises to which participants will be exposed, the sometimes lurid psychological upset they will witness, nor the fact that management is aware of at least some of the risks to which they subject participants."

REPORT OF THE APA TASK FORCE ON DECEPTIVE AND INDIRECT TECHNIQUES OF PERSUASION AND CONTROL, NOVEMBER 1986

CASE STUDIES: Intruding in the workplace

Specialist in cult activity and brainwashing Margaret Singer spent years studying the effects of LGATs, and was a professional witness in many lawsuits leveled against LGATs and the companies that forced their employees to attend LGAT courses. Her book *Cults in Our Midst* included these cases of individuals who suffered serious consequences:

CASE STUDY: Psychological breakdown

When "Gerald" applied for a management position, his prospective boss insisted he attend a particular LGAT seminar as a prerequisite for employment. His boss was a devotee of the group, which used a combination of New Age philosophy, guided imagery, confessions and confrontational attacks by the group leader. As each day went by, he became more anxious about way he felt forced to adopt a new philosophy. He felt himself falling apart psychologically, but the leaders insisted he stay – and he knew he would not get the job if he withdrew. On the fourth day of the course he was taken to a mental hospital and experienced a "brief reactive psychosis."

TAKE ⚠ CONTROL

Don't let your employer or anyone force you to attend an LGAT session. Get the consent of your doctor or counsellor before committing yourself to attend.

CASE STUDY: Psychological deterioration

Although "Joyce" was a top marketing executive in her firm, her supervisor recommended she attend a New Age training program in order to get ahead. She expected a work skills training program, but was surprised by the stressful methods she encountered. She was admitted to a psychiatric ward with almost continuous panic attacks. Although she had no prior history of panic attacks, she endured three years of debilitating phobias and panic disorders before she was able to resume normal employment.

CASE STUDY: Intense psychological stress

One company sent twelve female technical employees to an LGAT seminar. The women – who belonged to the same minority ethnic group – encountered an insensitive trainer who had formerly been employed as a security guard. He ran the program in the form of an attack therapy group and was unaware of the impact that the approach was causing. He had the women stand on a table at the front of the room while he criticized their bodies and clothing. All of the women experienced marked psychological stress and some resigned their positions shortly after. One of the women took her case to court and successfully claimed a settlement.

TAKE ⚠ CONTROL

If you feel un-comfortable at any point feel free to leave. Don't be embarrassed about exercising your free-dom of choice. It's the first real step to empowerment!

CASE STUDY: Training programs end in suicide attempts

"Jane" undertook two LGAT training programs in the late 1980s. She made the decision to share an experience in her past, where she was the victim of a brutal assault. Though she had not felt stigmatized by the experience, she was urged to "release" emotions associated with the assault. Even after exhibiting unusual side effects in her behavior, she was allowed to continue in the program, and felt that the trainers had singled her out for humiliation – having to endure embarrassing and degrading role-plays. She went into long-term depression which led to several suicide attempts. She was hospitalized for three years and successfully sued the corporation responsible for the program.

Source: "Cults in Our Midst," Margaret Singer

RESOURCE: Current white-collar cult research

Several groups monitor LGATs that drift into cult practices. As programs appear and disappear, changing their names and changing their staff, some organizations dedicate themselves to investigating complaints and researching the latest systems. Spend some time at these sites to familiarize yourself with the names and techniques that keep reoccurring as culprits.

FACT NET (www.factnet.org), EX CULT (www.ex-cult.org), "The Skeptic's Dictionary" (www.skepdic.com)

Motivational gurus use the Forer Effect to "connect" with individuals in the audience

Listen for these statements:

- "Do you want other people to like and admire you?"
- "You tend to be critical of yourself."
- "You have so much untapped potential."
- "You're held back by worry and insecurities."
- "You have too many doubts."
- "Don't be held back by limitations."
- "Do you want to change?"
- "Your goals are too unrealistic."

Sound familiar? Learn how the Forer Effect can give any speaker a "mystical" edge. >>

The Forer Effect

The Forer Effect (also known as the Barnum Effect) is used by clairvoyants, mind readers and astrologers, as well as motivational speakers. They say things that sound like they are meant for you in order to make you trust them.

B. R. Forer proved that most people accept particular statements as an accurate description of themselves, even when the statements can be applicable to anyone.

Forer gave a personality test to his students, ignored their answers and gave each student the following evaluation. He asked them to rate the evaluation from 0 to 5, with "5" meaning the recipient felt the evaluation was an "excellent" assessment and "4" meaning the assessment was "good." The class average evaluation was 4.26. That was in 1948. The test has been repeated hundreds of time with psychology students and the average is still around 4.2.

"You have a need for other people to like and admire you, and yet you tend to be critical of yourself. While you have some personality weaknesses you are generally able to compensate for them. You have considerable unused capacity that you have not turned to your advantage. Disciplined and self-controlled on the outside, you tend to be worrisome and insecure on the inside. At times you have serious doubts as to whether you have made the right decision or done the right thing. You prefer a certain amount of change and variety and become dissatisfied when hemmed in by restrictions and limitations. You also pride yourself as an independent thinker; and do not accept others' statements without satisfactory proof. But you have found it unwise to be too frank in revealing yourself to others. At times you are extroverted, affable, and sociable, while at other times you are introverted, wary, and reserved. Some of your aspirations tend to be rather unrealistic."

CLOSE-UP

Mass Meetings

The power of crowds to influence political change is one of the significant themes of history. Even the last twenty years have seen major crowds in Beijing, Berlin, Moscow and Seattle which have had historical impact. Persuasive politicians, religious gurus and activists can often resort to deceptive tactics to harness the power of crowds in order to advance their cause.

Leaderless protest crowds are another phenomenon having a powerful effect in politics. Major anti-globalization events in Seattle in 1999 and in London in 2001 were a turning point in the way that many governments view political protests. Protestors have deployed new communication technologies using laptop computers, the Internet and mobile SMS messages to organize. Some government agencies have responded with their own persuasive technology, including security camera networks and crowd management systems.

RESEARCH: Crowds and the individual

Gustave Le Bon (1841 - 1931) was a French psychologist whose many theories relating to the behavior of crowds are still recognized today.

He was born and studied medicine in France, and then toured Europe, Asia and North Africa while writing on archaeology and anthropology, before beginning his most famous works, on psychology – most notably *Les lois psychologiques de l'évolution des peuples* (1894; *The Psychology of Peoples*) and *La psychologie des foules* (1895; *The Crowd*). His main theories surrounded the tendencies for individuals to conform to the behavior of the group and towards exaggerated, extreme actions.

CLOSE-UP: Losing your "self" in the crowd

Gustav Le Bon developed many theories about crowd behavior that are still respected a century after he developed them.

This excerpt from "The Crowd" describes the bizarre change in personality that can occur in an individual when placed in a crowd.

"Man, as part of a multitude, is a very different being from the same man as an isolated individual. His conscious individuality vanishes in the unconscious personality of the crowd.

"Material contact is not absolutely necessary to produce in the individual the mentality of the crowd. Common passions and sentiments, provoked by certain events, are often sufficient to create it.

"The collective mind, momentarily formed, represents a very special kind of aggregate. Its chief peculiarity is that it is entirely dominated by unconscious elements, and is subject to a peculiar collective logic.

"Among the other characteristics of crowds, we must note their infinite credulity and exaggerated sensibility, their short-sightedness, and their incapacity to respond to the influences of reason. Affirmation, contagion, repetition and prestige constitute almost the only means of persuading them. Reality and experience have no effect upon them. The multitude will admit anything; nothing is impossible in the eyes of the crowd.

> **TAKE ⚠ CONTROL**
>
> **Check yourself when you are in a public crowd.** Are you true to your own character? How do your emotions change, and how do you express them?

"By reason of the extreme sensibility of crowds, their sentiments, good or bad, are always exaggerated. This exaggeration increases still further in times of revolution. The least excitement will then lead the multitude to act with the utmost fury. Their credulity, so great even in the normal state, is still further increased; the most improbable statements are accepted.

"...These various characteristics show that man in the crowd descends to a very low degree in the scale of civilization. He becomes a savage, with all a savage's faults and qualities, with all his momentary violence, enthusiasm, and heroism. In the intellectual domain a crowd is always inferior to the isolated unit. In the moral and sentimental domain it may be his superior. A crowd will commit a crime as readily as an act of abnegation.

Crowd Influence Toolkit

The unique dynamic of crowds lends itself to particular kinds of manipulation. Some religious and political rallies exploit these techniques. Keep your head and look out for these:

Induced Alpha State

Music, meditative practices, singing or sudden fright can induce a brain rhythm known as an Alpha State. For those who are not used to this experience, it will reduce critical thought and enable behavior suggestion.

Voice roll

A repeating vocal rhythm delivers words to a regular beat – this creates a hypnotic effect to open the way for subliminal suggestion. This technique sounds artificial when you hear it, but is regularly used. It sounds like the speaker is talking at length to an imaginery beat. It may be used by religious speakers and politicians.

"True believer" manipulation

In any given crowd, a significant percentage are unusually susceptible to suggestion. Such people may be acting out of fear or gullibility, but are easily manipulated by the speaker. They may be the first to cry, laugh, agree to or follow the speaker's instructions. Their behavior may have a flow-on effect to surrounding people in the audience.

> **TAKE ⚠ CONTROL**
> Take a friend along. Talk over these tactics before you arrive at a large meeting or religious rally.

The "yes set"

The "yes set" is when the speaker sets up a series of "yes" questions and closes them with a false conclusion.

"Do you love your country? Yes! Do you love your family? Yes! Do you want more freedom? Yes! Then vote Jerry Smith in as your next President!"

TAKE ⚠️ **CONTROL**

Listen carefully.
If a speaker starts to employ well known gestures or vocal techniques make a mental note of the message being projected or concealed.

An identical effect can be created, using a "no set."

Manipulative hand gestures

Speakers can use gestures to mask, reinforce or override the meaning of the words being said. Communication occurs largely through the use of nonverbal expression. If you're looking for the speaker's message, don't listen to the words – only 7% of the meaning can be found there.

Particular hand and arm gestures can be coordinated with speech to project subliminal signals by distracting the observers and interrupting normal verbal comprehension. More than 70% of communication is non-verbal. Most manipulative gestures are made with the left hand, with the right hand out of sight. These gestures stimulate your right brain functions, allowing the speaker to tap into your emotions and visual regions of your brain.

1. One gesture conveys authority. The hand is shaped into a tight, tiny fist, but the thumb is straight up on the side of the fist, tightly clamped against the fingers on the side, with the edge of the thumb running parallel to the TOP of the back of the hand.

2. Another popular gesture is designed to conceal a dishonest statement. The fingers are straight and close together, with the palm cupped and the thumb held tightly to the side of the fingers.

Actions Speak Louder Than Words

Voice Expression 38%

Words 7%

Gestures, Face and Body 55%

Psychologists Alton Barbour and Mele Koneya explained the relative importance of gestures in the book "Louder Than Words"

3. This one conveys generosity and may be used to conceal greed. The speaker places his hand close to his body, just below the breast, then moves the hand up and outward.

4. Gathering - attention focus. The hands open reaching to the left and then the right in a gathering motion.

5. Fingers and thumb curl inwards as if loosely grasping an object. A mild power grip, usually employed by a person saying something without great force of convinction, but who nevertheless wishes to be taken seriously.

6. Power grips show a speaker's wish to make a point with strength or to control the audience. Fingers and thumb make a tightly closed fist. A forceful power grip signals conviction and determination – usually deliberately exploited by public speakers, priests and politicians who might in reality have neither.

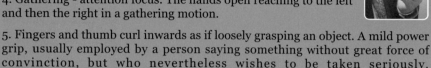

Embedded commands

Suggestions that carry a strong emphasis that affects the listener, and provokes a sympathetic emotional response. E.g., "Aren't you sick and tired of being overweight?" or "This place is driving me crazy!" These statements presuppose a positive response, and the listener can easily be caught off guard, agreeing to something unintentionally.

Other Neurolinguistic Programming techniques use repetition, word association and phrase sequencing tricks to persuade the listener to agree. One common example is the nested presupposition, e.g. "Do you need any further evidence before you vote for this man?" - where the speaker imposes a choice on the listeners.

TAKE ⚠ CONTROL

Mainstream religious organizations sometimes resort to manipulative techniques.
Learn to discriminate between legitimate orthodox practices and cult tactics.

Vibrato rhythm and E.L.F.

Sound waves of various frequencies can affect human physiology and the brain, producing involuntary actions. (Extra-low frequency waves have been reported to produce feelings of depression or euphoria depending on the speed of the waves. Some opera soloists have been known to evoke unusual physiological effects when singing certain notes.

A patented device for "Subliminal acoustic manipulation of nervous systems" is one of many new players in this field. It is unlikely such devices are in wide use, but it is impossible to know for sure.

Love bombing

Creating an intensively positive emotional mood for a short period of time in order to elicit a false feeling of goodwill or excitement. This tactic may be used by religious leaders or gurus, who orchestrate love bombing amongst followers to captivate enquiring outsiders. It creates a false emotional environment that can be magnetic and addictive.

The Forer Effect

The Forer or Barnum Effect (outlined in the Motivational Seminars section) is a technique used by a speaker to create a "connection" with the audience. Using vague statements that could apply to anyone, but that sound personalized, gives an impression of authority or mystical knowledge.

US Patent: 6,017,302

Subliminal acoustic manipulation of nervous systems

"In human subjects, sensory resonances can be excited by subliminal atmospheric acoustic pulses that are tuned to the resonance frequency... The effects of the 2.5 Hz resonance include slowing of certain cortical processes, sleepiness, and disorientation. For these effects to occur, the acoustic intensity must lie in a certain deeply subliminal range. Suitable apparatus consists of a portable battery-powered source of weak subaudio acoustic radiation... There is further application as a nonlethal weapon that can be used in law enforcement standoff situations, for causing drowsiness and disorientation in targeted subjects. It is then preferable to use venting acoustic monopoles in the form of a device that inhales and exhales air with subaudio frequency."

This patent notice describes a device which can be used to manipulate an audience by using inaudible sound waves.

Further mind-changing patented devices are listed in an appendix to this book.

"Personal characteristics vanish in the crowd, which exerts an extraordinary influence upon the individuals which form it. The miser becomes generous, the skeptic a believer, the honest man a criminal, the coward a hero. Examples of such transformations abounded during the great Revolution.

"As part of a jury or a parliament, the collective man renders verdicts or passes laws of which he would never have dreamed in his isolated condition.

"One of the most notable consequences of the influence of a collectivity upon the individuals who compose it is the unification of their sentiments and wills. This psychological unity confers a remarkable force upon crowds.

"The formation of such a mental unity results chiefly from the fact that in a crowd gestures and actions are extremely contagious. Acclamations of hatred, fury, or love are immediately approved and repeated.

"What is the origin of these common sentiments; this common will? They are propagated by contagion, but a point of departure is necessary before this contagion can take effect."

DEFINITION: Deindividuation

Deindividuation describes the loss of self awareness than occurs to individuals in a crowd. This explains the tendency to shout, laugh, clap, cheer or become caught up in the emotion of the moment. Mob rule, herd mentality, the group mind  and mass hysteria are other states that are related to deindividuation.

DOCUMENT: Recipe for mass protests

Mass protests can be instigated and controlled by a relatively small number of individuals. A CIA manual outlined one technique used in overpowering the government of Nicaragua in the 1980s. It can be carried out by means of the infiltration of a small group of guerrillas who will have the mission of agitating, giving the impression that there are many of them and that they have popular backing. Using the tactics of a force of 200-300 agitators, a demonstration can be created in which 10,000-20,000 persons take part.

From "CIA PSYCHOLOGICAL OPERATIONS IN GUERRILLA WARFARE."

REPORT: Hidden technology and crowd persuasion

One report has highlighted the advanced methods now being used to control protest crowds. "What is emerging in certain quarters is a chilling picture of ongoing innovation in the science and technology of social and political control, including: semi-intelligent zone-denial systems using neural networks which can identify and potentially punish unsanctioned behavior; the advent of global telecommunications surveillance systems using voice recognition and other biometric techniques to facilitate

TAKE !
CONTROL
Find out about your local police policy on protest marches. Talk to activist groups and find out whether police tactics are hindering democratic freedom.

human tracking; data-veillance systems which can match computer held data to visual recognition systems or identify friendship maps simply by analyzing the telephone and email links between who calls whom; new sub-lethal incapacitating weapons used both for prison and riot control as well as in sub-state conflict operations other than war; new target acquisition aids, lethal weapons and expanding dum-dum like ammunition which although banned by the Geneva conventions for use against other states' soldiers, is finding increasing popularity amongst SWAT and special forces teams; discreet order vehicles designed to look like ambulances on prime time television but which can deploy a formidable array of weaponry to provide a show of force in countries like Indonesia or Turkey, or spray harassing chemicals or dye onto protesters. Such marking appears to be kid-glove in its restraint but tags all protesters so that the snatch squads can arrest them later, out of the prying lenses of CNN."

AN APPRAISAL OF THE TECHNOLOGIES OF POLITICAL CONTROL

An Omega Foundation Summary & Options Report for the European Parliament

SEPTEMBER 1998

The novel *1984,* written by George Orwell in 1948, predicted use of surveillance as a means of coercive control.

Every citizen, or at least every citizen important enough to be worth watching, could be kept twenty-four hours a day under the eyes of the police and in the sound of official propaganda, with all other channels of communication closed. The possibility of enforcing not only complete obedience to the will of the State, but complete uniformity of opinion of all subjects now existed.

GEORGE ORWELL

1984

More about security cameras and privacy at **www.observingsurveillance.org**

CROWD CONTROL

"What is emerging in certain quarters is a chilling picture of ongoing innovation in the science and technology of social and political control, including: semi-intelligent zone-denial systems using neural networks which can identify and potentially punish unsanctioned behavior; the advent of global telecommun-ications surveillance systems using voice recognition and other biometric techniques to facilitate human tracking."

Report for the European Parliament on Crowd Management Technology
September 1998

TACTIC: Camera surveillence and passive coercion

Sophisticated CCTV cameras are now equipped to detect non-conforming behavior and crowd dynamics and transmit them to security personnel and government. If you belong to a minority religious or political group, you may be in for some extra attention. Government monitoring is now used to manage protest crowd movements and record individuals' faces.

**TAKE !
CONTROL**
Follow the security policy of your local government. Be wary of promises of increased security. These claims are rarely backed by detailed evidence.

TREND: Security camera network used as control device

The British program CACTUS (Command and Control Training and Planning Using Knowledge Based Simulation) allows the incident commander to operate remotely, hundreds of miles away from the actual street disorder. All the information from the CCTV cameras in the streets and on helicopters is fed in through fiber optic lines, collated and then filtered. Once compiled with tactical reports from the street, the system allows the operator to issue live commands which drip back down the command chain to the individual police officer in the street. These officers have a special communication system built straight into their riot helmets which only allows them to receive commands.

TACTIC: Microwave technology disperses crowds

New invisible weapons are being deployed in the attempt to control protest crowds. Some protesters are concerned about the introduction of long range non-lethal weapons known as "People Zappers" that deliver a burning electromagnetic ray to the skin without leaving a mark. A US airforce Vehicle Mounted Active Denial Technology (VMAD) uses a transmitter to send a narrow beam of energy towards an identified subject. "Traveling at the speed of light, the energy reaches the subject and penetrates less than 1/64 of an inch into the skin, quickly heating up the skin's surface." Some human rights groups have complained that this is outside the boundary of acceptable crowd control tactics.

TACTIC: Leaderless collectives influence large groups

Protest groups at anti-WTO gatherings have developed a system known as Coordinated Decentralization. Leaders of hundreds of small groups build numbers using SMS text messages, email and websites. This enables mass gatherings of thousands to form and disperse rapidly, or take part in sporadic smaller protests according to their preference.

CLOSE-UP

Stadiums and Sport

An excited crowd makes for a psychologically compliant audience. The rush by big brand names to slap their logo on everything from the local stadium to the bare skin of players reveals the magnetic power of the arena. The daily spectacle of sporting events has attracted new interest with company's recognizing that the scoreboard, umpire and playing field are all fair game. The weekly ballgame is incidental to the billion dollar struggle of corporations competing for the attention of the fans.

TREND: Sports Lovers v. Big Money

Sports enthusiasts have fought a losing battle for many years against the use of their sport for commercial purposes. The battle has gone to a new level in recent years.

From sports apparel companies buying college athletic programs, to the commercial intrusion into high school sports by corporations looking for the next superstar, to the sale of naming rights of our publicly-funded stadiums and arenas to the highest corporate bidder, sports fans are drowning in an ocean of commercialism. It is reaching the point, in our professional and college sports, where advertising is the program or attraction, and the games are reduced to clutter.

TAKE CONTROL

Support your local stadium or arena. Encourage fans and friends to write to local politicians and media to help prevent local sports fields being re-named by businesses.

TACTIC: Stadium branding enables sponsored conversation

Ralph Nader led a forceful protest against the renaming of Metropolitan Football Stadium – pointing out that this kind of corporate branding results in branded conversations: "This is not just about a stadium name. This is about whether we might have physical and mental space that is not cluttered by corporate logos nor colonized by the materialistic, self-serving, money-is-everything values of the market. We are drowning in an ocean of commercialism. We are buried under junk mail, telemarketing, junk faxes and billboards. We are barraged with ads in airport lounges, bus stops, doctors' offices, movie theaters, hospitals, gas stations, elevators, convenience stores, on the Internet, on fruit, beach sand, garbage cans, ATMs and countless other places. Even worse, our public schools have become showrooms for the delivery of ads to captive audiences of impressionable children. And our elections have been commercialized and corrupted by huge sums of corporate 'soft money' campaign contributions."

www.leagueoffans.org

TAKE ⚠ CONTROL

Contact the fans of your local team. Write to players and board members of your team urging them to take a stand against commercialism in sport.

TACTIC: Sports stadiums capture "dwell time."

Crowds attending live sporting events are subjected to a commercial barrage unlike any other. It is impossible to look anywhere without viewing a sponsor's logo. A company called Stadia is making money by putting advertising on the backs of seats. "The long dwell time accompanied by the chance for product sampling or to take away details on the bag makes this an attractive proposition for a variety of advertisers," said a spokesman for the company.

The Guardian

TREND: Publicity stunts "hijack" audiences

High profile international sporting events are attracting fame-seekers who interrupt an event with a stunt knowing that 100 million viewers are watching them – some carry corporate logos on their bare skin.

A streaker painted with a large Vodafone logo interrupted a major Rugby match in Sydney, Australia. The incident was broadcast live on television and received front page news coverage the following day, resulting in substantial free publicity for Vodafone.

NAMING RIGHTS

"This is not just about a stadium name. This is about whether we might have physical and mental space that is not cluttered by corporate logos nor colonized by the materialistic, self-serving, money-is-everything values of the market. We are drowning in an ocean of commercialism."

Ralph Nader

FEDEX FIELD, Raljon
$205 million for 27 years

AMERICAN AIRLINES CENTER, Dallas
$195 million for 30 years

CMGi Field, Foxborough
$120 million for 15 years

STAPLES CENTER, Los Angeles
$100 million for 20 years

ENRON FIELD, Houston
$100 million for 30 years

YOUR NAME HERE

The CEO of Vodafone distanced himself from the incident, and the motive for the stunt remains a mystery. Regardless of how it was instigated, it resulted in a massive branding blitz for Vodafone at minimal expense.

RESOURCE: Speaking up for the fans

The League of Fans website keeps track of the ever increasing schemes to leverage the medium of sport. Founded by Ralph Nader, it organizes petitions and media action against corruption in college sport, commercial intrusion into high school sport, sponsorship saturation – promoting the rights of fans. "Sports fans across the country have become bitter because money, ads and hype are draining the fun out of sports. Even worse, what we pay for with our hard-earned dollars is the further degradation of culture and deterioration of the games we love, while commercial values are introduced and reinforced to new generations of sports fans."

www.leagueoffans.org

TREND: Athletes selling skin for corporate ads

To capitalize on the growing trend of tattoo-wearing by NBA players, corporations are now offering large sums to individual players to have their corporate logos tattooed onto players' bodies. While the NBA's collective bargaining agreement prohibits players from signing deals to place corporate advertisements on their uniforms, it makes no mention of placing ads on the exposed skin of players. But even though tattoos aren't explicitly addressed, NBA rules prohibit commercialization on the court beyond the uniform manufacturer's logos.

"It's like freedom of speech is like something that no one can tell me what I can do to my own body. This is my own domain. This is my own kingdom... So, I'm proud of it, and, you know, if somebody's watching, bring it on, and the check too, so we can talk about it."

www.leagueoffans.org

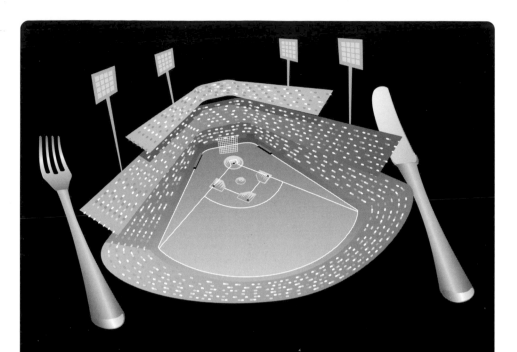

"The sports industry has allowed itself to be dominated by corporations looking to own or control our culture. We, as fans and taxpayers have been forced into a situation where the teams we love and the politicians we elect allow marketers to buy or lay claim to every moment of our attention."

LEAGUE OF FANS

TACTIC: Virtual advertising

A technology, dubbed as "virtual advertising" or "virtual signage," has exploded onto the sports marketing scene showing an unlimited potential for ad placement.

Developed by a company called Princeton Video Image (PVI), this advertising breakthrough uses the same technology that creates game enhancements such as the virtual first down line on televised football games. Using this virtual advertising technology, an ad can be electronically placed anywhere in a stadium or on a playing surface, making it look like the ad is actually a sign or painted onto the surface to a person watching on television, without actually physically existing in that stadium. We commonly see this now in baseball, from the center field shot of pitcher vs. batter, with a virtual ad on the wall behind home plate. It's increasingly used in all of the other major sports as well.

"League of Fans is motivated by people, just like you, who are fed up with what the sports industry has become and want to do something about it. We work with concerned citizens, sports fans, civic groups and communities to increase awareness of the sports industry's relationship to society and influence a broad range of issues in sports at all levels."

www.leagueoffans.org

TACTIC: Crowds + Sport = Beer

Bids for exclusive sponsorship of the National Football League increase each year as major beer brands battle for the rights to connect their logo with the sport. Beer has always been the ultimate product tie-in for any sport, and now companies intend to maximize every second that their name appears in the stadium and television broadcasts. Although there has long been an association with alcohol and violence at sporting events, the revenues from beer sponsorship and sales are too great to refuse. The emotion and excitement generated by sporting events provides a proven strategy for a brand to be permanently etched on the drinker's mind.

INSIDER SECRET: Stadium pouring rights

Captive audiences are getting less say in what they eat and drink thanks to stadium managers and the major beverage brands. By securing exclusive "stadium pouring rights" for millions of dollars, a company can ensure that you only drink *their* brand. One stadium even hindered fans from drinking water by designing their stadium without water fountains. A citizens' protest pressured the management into having them installed.

Cashing in on cheers and keeping score

"Like so many other venues for mass communication, today's sports spectacles are desperately looking for new ways to appeal to all of their potential audiences. A well-designed spectacle has the power to unify tens of thousands of different people into a single, cheering mass. However the energy of the mob may have been directed in the past—toward particular political, religious, or cultural ideologies—today an afternoon at the Meadowlands has been fine-tuned to elicit our allegiance to the corporations sponsoring the game. The emotionally aroused spectators are exposed to commercial messages nonstop. Corporate logos adorn every available surface— the walls, a blimp overhead, the water coolers, the turnstiles, even the tickets. Every time we look up to check the stats, we are reminded who really keeps score: the half-dozen corporations whose logos alternately loom over the scoreboard.

The timing of commercial interruptions is meant to capitalize on the cresting emotional states of the crowd. At the conclusion of particularly exciting or narrowly decided plays, an announcer with an amplified, God-like voice calls our attention to huge state-of-the-art video screens. After watching a two-second commercial message ("This instant replay is brought to you by..."), we are treated to video recap framed within a corporate logo. It is with desperate and rapt attention that the crowd beholds the video image. Our critical faculties are suspended during these moments of heightened passion. That's why they cost the most for a company to sponsor." —Coercion

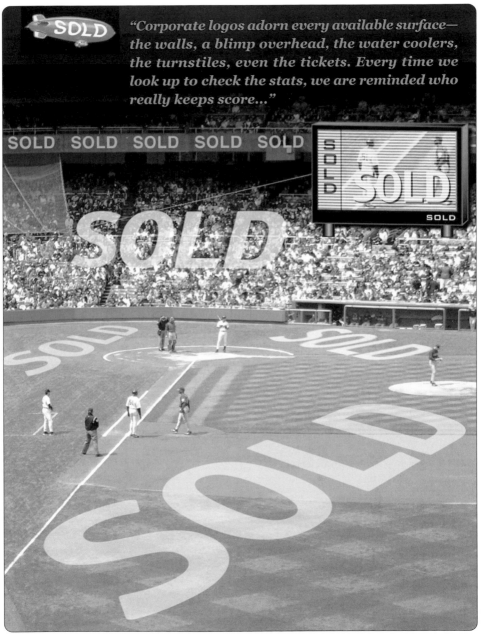

"Corporate logos adorn every available surface—the walls, a blimp overhead, the water coolers, the turnstiles, even the tickets. Every time we look up to check the stats, we are reminded who really keeps score..."

The Media Zone

"...it is now possible to control and regiment the masses according to our will without their knowing it."

EDWARD BERNAYS, The "Father" of Public Relations

We Know What You Want
Chapter 3: **The Media Zone**

We rely on the media to find out what is going
on in our world, our country and our community.
There's never been a larger network of journalists
around the globe with the technology to
communicate their reports, yet TV news is
becoming less diverse. Newspapers are carrying
more sponsored editorials than ever. Our
decisions and beliefs are informed by voices
driven by a profit motive.

In this chapter:

- **Who chooses your news?**
- **How PR influences society**
- **Modern government propaganda**
- **Hidden messages in media**
- **Engineering opinion**
- **Manipulating young minds**

CLOSE-UP

Television

Documercials, placements, secret branding and sponsored conversations are replacing genuine TV content and information. Concentrating media ownership results in censoring the number of objective voices.

Most people now rely on television as their primary source of information. The combination of business pressures and shifting ethical standards has eroded the quality of information offered, while making it more appealing. The result is an ill-informed public manipulated by subliminal tactics.

"Professional electronic journalists should: Clearly disclose the origin of information and label all material provided by outsiders."
Radio-Television News Directors Association Code of Ethics

REPORT: TV news analysis

1 Hour of CNN Yields Less Than 5 Minutes of News: Information comes at a price. In this study, CNN provided 55 minutes of filler material to entertain viewers in one hour of its widely respected news program. News information was diluted with opinion pieces, infomercials and tabloid gossip items. A detailed analysis by TvNewsLies.org is:

CNN, September 5th 2003 - 7PM EST

Real News	4.75 minutes
Talk Show Content	5.75 minutes
Headlines	6.50 minutes
Regional News	7.50 minutes
Tabloid Stories	14.25 minutes
Infomercial Content	8.5 minutes
Commercial Advertising	12.75 minutes

TAKE ⚠ CONTROL

Conduct your own analysis of the news you watch.

TREND: Fake news items

Real news items are being replaced by slick corporate promotions and goverment messages. Video News Releases (VNRs) prepared and supplied by corporations and governments are slotted into evening bulletins.VNRs secretly promote pharmaceuticals, government programs, medical information and public service messages. Newsrooms save time and money by running VNRs reducing staff costs and studio production fees. According to a recent Nielsen Media Research Survey, about 80 percent of U.S. news directors air VNRs several times a month, and 100 percent of American television newsrooms now use VNRs in their newscasts.

TAKE !
CONTROL
Watch closely for VNRs. If your local network is running them, alert them to real stories in your community.

CASE STUDY: MediaLink

The MediaLink corporate site proclaims the success and prevalence of VNRs. "Pioneered professionally by MediaLink, the Video News Release (VNR), the television version of the printed press release, translates the printed word into the sound and pictures television newsrooms need. Produced in broadcast news style, VNRs relay the news of a product launch, medical discovery, corporate merger event, timely feature or breaking news to television news decision-makers. Every major television station in the world now uses VNRs regularly, and most are from Medialink. It's a fact."

www.medialink.com

CASE STUDY: MediaBlitz®

TVA productions offers a Public Relations product called MediaBlitz®, which "promises to get your story placed on our network of 1,100 TV stations, 40 major airlines (in-flight programming), 6,600 radio stations, 10,250 newspapers, 400 magazines & journals, and thousands of news portals. We have a team of over 140 people including a large Media Relations Department to maintain our carefully cultivated contacts in our database and to keep track of which formats broadcasters and editors need – and their editorial calendars... And we offer the strongest track record and guarantees in the industry." Successes include a blitz that resulted in

How *they* choose your news.

Global Newswire services select hundreds of major stories

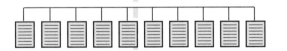

Network Editors select 6-10 stories for the national broadcast based on which ones will attract the most viewers.

Global News items are combined with junk news and paid content and broadcast to your home.

Video News Releases

VNR

Cash-strapped newsrooms are turning to free pre-recorded "news items" to save money – pushing real stories off the agenda. Broadcasters are not required to advise viewers that they are viewing paid VNRs, which are regularly used by drug companies, biotech firms and Industry Front Groups.

NEW TREND

ONE COMPANY GUARANTEES to get your company massive news coverage nationwide in both the U.S. and Canada, on up to 20,000 media outlets. It will create and distribute ready-made Feature Releases on your company, product, service or cause in a format broadcasters and editors can easily use immediately. Our veteran producers, directors, writers and editors (including former CNN and top daily newspaper and wire service editors) will develop the plan to your approval, implement it and measure the results.

JUNK NEWS	REAL NEWS	VNRs

NIGHTLY NEWS CONTENT

company VSNIs share price nearly tripling. SCAN, a senior citizens' lobby group, confirmed that TVA was instrumental in getting new national legislation passed. Spotlights aired intensively in Washington D.C. while the bill in question was being considered by Congress. The TVA website claims that over 20,000 TV, radio and print media outlets have come to rely on their ready-made news features to meet their own growing need for editorial content due to staff cutbacks.

www.tvaproductions.com

Timing bad news for the "right" moment

A leaked memo from a political adviser to Stephen Byers, the UK transport secretary, suggests that the government should take advantage of the world crisis to bury any controversial decisions. This memo from Jo Moore, who was also Mr Byers' adviser at the Department of Industry, was sent as email within half an hour of the second plane hitting the twin towers in New York on September 11.

"It's now a very good day to get out anything we want to bury. Councillors expenses? Jo"

The Guardian, October 10, 2001

FOCUS: Which stories get left out?

Each day hundreds of important stories are left out of the evening news. There may be no video available for them, or they may not be sufficiently entertaining for the viewing audience. Such stories (though they are important) lead to lower ratings and reduced income to TV stations. Each night there is only time for four or five international news stories. If you were a news editor; which ones would you leave out from this list?

___ Oil spill threatens Reef Island
___ United Nations votes to uphold ban on torture
___ Japan stocks fall 5%
___ Environment summit
___ Palestinian leader arrested
___ Bus plunge in China, 20 dead
___ New AIDS treatment developed in Scotland
___ Indian leader threatens Pakistan
___ Space probe reaches Jupiter

Get your own "News Scorecard" at gradethenews.org

TAKE ⚠ **CONTROL**

Don't rely on TV news for an accurate view of the world. Use a combination of resources such as those suggested at the web site for this book.

THEORY: Manufacturing Consent

Manufacturing Consent - *The Political Economy of the Mass Media* by Noam Chomsky and Edward Herman argues that, since large corporations now run mass media news outlets, they are under the same competitive pressures as other corporations. According to the book, the pressure to create a stable, profitable business invariably biases the kinds of news items reported, as well as the manner and emphasis in which they are reported, and these biases occur despite the best efforts of the reporters and editors to fairly report all the newsworthy events. The book further points out issues with the dependency of mass media news outlets upon major sources of news, particularly the government. If a particular outlet is in disfavor with a government, it can be "shut out," and other outlets given preferential treatment. Since this results in a loss in news leadership, it can also result in a loss of readership/viewership. That can thereby result in a loss of advertising revenue, which is the primary income for most mass media (newspapers, magazines, television).

TAKE CONTROL

Observe the way that governement news is reported. Assess the relationships between media and government as it is explained in books by Chomsky and others.

From Wikipedia

TREND: Media concentration affects accuracy

Objectivity requires different perspectives on the news, and different views of our world. The number of viewpoints is rapidly decreasing, as competing networks run the same news items in similar order with the same footage. This is compounded by cultural and political bias. A handful of multinational corporations control nearly everything we see and hear on the screen, over the airwaves and in print. Subtle threats to freedom of expression come from within media as a result of media concentration, globalization and a culture of greed within the industry. The major networks regularly project a single dominant viewpoint on complex issues such as Middle East conflict, racial tension and medical science. This is a powerful means of persuasion.

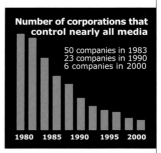

Number of corporations that control nearly all media

50 companies in 1983
23 companies in 1990
6 companies in 2000

1980   1985   1990   1995   2000

www.mediachannel.org/ownership

TACTIC: Commercials imitate news breaks

News breaks that highlighted breakthrough medications turned out to be paid advertisements for big drug companies. Since they are slotted in between real TV programs, viewers are led to believe they are watching a scheduled newscast. Aaron Brown of CNN, Walter Cronkite and other broadcast journalists were hired to appear in videos resembling news items from "American Medical Review" paid for by drug makers and other healthcare companies, blurring the line between journalism and advertising. The producers, WJMK Inc. charged drug companies around $15,000 to have their products featured.

TACTIC: Digital product placement

Virtual placement uses digital imaging to place products into TV shows that were never there to begin with. An episode of UPN's *Seven Days* had four name-brand products or logos artificially added after the fact – a can of Coca-Cola, a bottle of Evian, a Kenneth Cole bag and a Wells Fargo Bank sign. "It was done as a test on a rerun," says UPN spokesman Paul Maguire. "Now we're evaluating the official response." Similar techniques are used to superimpose ads on sports fields for telecasts.

TACTIC: Sponsored conversations on talk shows

Talk shows are beginning to feature scripted conversations where hosts slip in product names and sponsored information.

During a recent "bachelor party" segment for host Tom Arnold, one of the guests was a relatively unknown actor from a Dockers commercial. In a staged interaction, Arnold splashed his drink on the actor's pants in mock anger, then talked about the Dockers Go Khaki Stain Defender pants' ability to withstand staining.

The pressure on TV shows to offset costs by embedding paid endorsements means any on air conversation could become a secret sales pitch.

TAKE ⚠ CONTROL

Be an *active* TV viewer. Be alert to embedded endorsements. Write to television stations who don't disclose hidden endorsements.

CASE STUDY: Sponsors sneak into sitcoms

Brand names are the new parasites on TV shows. A quick line about Cinnabon popped up in the middle of a popular sitcom – but it was no accident. Writers were told to insert the brand name as part of the show. Now fans aren't sure which segments are sales pitch and which are ad-free. Cinnabon received a verbal mention and a hands-on placement during NBC's hit comedy series *Will & Grace*, starring Debra Messing and Eric McCormack. In the scene, Will (McCormack) is sitting in his office with Grace (Messing) waiting for Jack McFarland (Sean Hayes). Jack soon enters the office eating a Cinnabon roll and says, "Sorry I'm late. The meeting ran a little long." Will asks, "What meeting?" Jack answers, "In that room down the hall. I don't know what they were yammering about, but they had Cinnabons and coffee. It was good. We got a lot done." This episode of the show reached an audience of over 30 million viewers.

www.acreativegroup.com

TREND: Interactive TV builds lifestyle profiles

TAKE CONTROL

Ask your interactive TV provider for their privacy statement to find out how your information will be shared.

With people spending up to 25% of their week in front of the television, interactive television gives media companies extensive data on people's private lives. It has been designed from the beginning to gather information about people in their own homes. Using the TV's return path and artificial intelligence, interactive TV providers do demographic, lifestyle, market segmentation and psychographic analysis of your viewing habits. Such analyses can be combined with externally available data to create an intimate picture of who you are and what motivates you. *White Dot* has been investigating this new technology for three years. "Spy TV was written as a concise viewer's guide to the hardware, the software, and the privacy issues of this new medium. Based on dozens of interviews with interactive television developers in Britain and America, Spy TV cuts through the hype of this 'digital revolution...' "

www.whitedot.org/spyinteractive/faqs.htm

TREND: Governments exploit media desperation

When governments need to influence public opinion, they can count on news organizations to take up sensational stories whether they are true or not. In 1990, PR Firm, "Hill and Knowlton on behalf of the Citizens for a Free Kuwait front group of exiled royals, produced a 15-year-old girl 'Nayirah' who testified that she saw Iraqi troops committing the atrocity in a Kuwaiti hospital. She testified before the Congressional Human Rights caucus in Oct. 1990 that Iraqis took 15 babies from incubators, which they then stole, and left premature infants 'on the cold floor to die'... Fitz-Pegado provided media coaching skills to Nayirah, who as it turned out, was the daughter of Kuwait's Ambassador to the U.S., and had never visited the hospital."

O'Dwyer's PR Daily

RESOURCE: Corporate interference in journalism

Into the Buzzsaw is a collection of reports by award-winning journalists who have been prevented from publishing major stories.

"The contributors reveal the dangerous state of American journalism. Writing in riveting, often gut-wrenching detail about their personal experiences with the 'buzzsaw' – concerted corporate and/or government efforts to kill their controversial stories and their careers – the contributors reveal the awesome depth and breadth of censorship in America today."

www.intothebuzzsaw.com

"The low cost of video production and the increase in available channels gave rise to countless tabloid television shows. Like their print counterparts, these programs broadcast stories that more established news agencies would have held back which in turn gave rise to a whole new set of journalistic standards and an unleashing of alternative news sources and outlets. Tabloid and Internet journalists were the first to publish everything from Clinton's trysts with Gennifer Flowers and Monica Lewinsky to Prince Charles' dirty phone calls with Camilla Parker-Bowles. *Time* and *Newsweek* have simply struggled to keep up with the rising tide." —*Coercion*

CLOSE-UP
Newspapers

Media ownership, sponsored editorial and layout tricks determine what we read and what is censored.

William Randolph Hearst recognized the entertainment potential of sensationalized news in the 1930s. Ever since then, newspapers have leveraged the layout of the newspaper to reflect editorial priorities of their publishers. Now many dailies are at a turning point, where ethical standards are buckling beneath the weight of commercial pressures. Editors are submitting to government intimidation and journalists are being made redundant by cost saving pre-written press releases.

"People don't actually read newspapers,
they step into them like a warm bath."
- Marshall McLuhan

TACTIC: How a news layout works

Newspaper editors decide what stories are the most important each day. Would you make the same choices? Number the list below. Which story would you lead with? Which would you put inside the paper and which would you leave out?

___ United Nations votes to uphold ban on torture

___ Japan stocks fall 5%

___ Police suspect charged

___ Environmental summit sees historic breakthrough

___ Palestinian leader arrested

___ Bus plunge in China, 20 dead

Daily Times

Police charge suspect

Hos ediscit et hos arto stipata [...] spectat Rom[...] et hos num[...] as ad nost[...] Livi scrip[...] aevo. Interdu[...] rectum videt, est ubi peccat. Si veteres ita miratur laudatque poetas, ut nihil anteferat, nihil illis comparet, errat. Si quaedam nimis antique, si peraque dure dicere credit eos, ignave multa fatetur, et sapit et mecum facit et Iova iudicat aequo.

Non equidem insector delendave carmina Livi esse reor, memini quae plagosum mihi parvo Orbilium dictare; sed emendata videri pulchraque et exactis minimum distantia miror. Inter quae verbum emicuit si forte decorum, et si versus paulo concinnior unus et alter, iniuste totum ducit venditque poema.

Si meliora dies, ut vina, poemata reddit, scire velim, chartis pretium quotus arroget annus. scriptor abhinc annos centum qui decidit, inter perfectos veteresque referri debet an inter vilis atque novos? Excludat iurgia finis, "Est vetus

atque probus, centum qui perficit annos." Quid, qui deperiit minor uno mense vel anno, inter quos referendus erit? Veteresne poetas, an quos et praesens et postera resquat aetas?

"Iste quidem veteres inter ponetur honeste, qui vel mense brevi vel toto est iunior anno." Utor permisso, caudaeque pilos ut equinae paulatim vello unum, demo etiam unum, dum cadat elusus ratione ruentis acervi, qui redit in fastos et virtutem aestimat annis miraturque nihil nisi

Si meliora dies, ut vina, poemata reddit, scire velim, chartis pretium quotus arroget annus. scriptor abhinc annos centum qui

---

Hos ediscit et hos arto stipata theatro spectat Roma potens; habet hos numeratque poetas ad nostrum tempus Livi scriptoris ab aevo. Interdum volgus rectum videt, est ubi peccat. Si veteres ita miratur laudatque poetas, ut nihil anteferat, nihil illis comparet, errat. Si quaedam nimis antique, si peraque dure dicere credit eos, ignave multa fatetur, et sapit et mecum facit et Iova iudicat aequo.

Non equidem insector delendavecarmina Livi esse reor, memini quae plagosum mihi parvo Orbilium dictare; sed emendata videri pulchraque et exactis minimum distantia miror. Inter quae verbum emicuit si forte decorum, et si versus paulo concinnior unus et alter, iniuste totum ducit venditque poema.

Si meliora dies, ut vina, poemata reddit, scire velim, chartis

Environmental summit sees historic breakthrough

Hos ediscit et hos arto stipata theatro spectat Roma potens; habet hos numeratque poetas ad nostrum tempus Livi scriptoris ab aevo. Interdum volgus

rectum videt, est ubi peccat. Si veteres ita miratur laudatque poetas, ut nihil anteferat, nihil illis comparet, errat. Si quaedam nimis

antiq[...]ue ignave [...]os, sapit et [...]et Iova iudic[...]aequo.

Non equidem insector

Shuttle lift-off delayed due to weather

Hos ediscit et hos arto stipata theatro spectat Roma potens; habet hos numeratque poetas ad nostrum tempus Livi scriptoris ab aevo. Interdum volgus rectum videt, est ubi peccat. Si veteres ita miratur laudatque poetas, ut nihil anteferat, nihil illis comparet, errat. Si quaedam nimis antique, si peraque dure dicere credit eos, ignave multa

fatetur, et sapit et mecum facit et Iova iudicat aequo.

Non equidem insector delendave carmina Livi esse [...]mini quae pla[...]e; sed em[...]ideri pulc[...]exactis mini[...]distantia miror. Inter quae verbum emicuit si forte decorum, et si versus paulo concinnior unus et alter,

iniuste totum ducit venditque poema.

Si meliora dies, ut vina, poemata reddit, scire velim, chartis pretium quotus arroget annus. scriptor abhinc annos centum qui decidit, inter perfectos veteresque referri debet an inter vilis atque novos? Excludat iurgia finis, "Est vetus atque probus, centum qui perficit annos." Quid, qui

deperiit minor uno mense vel anno, inter quos referendus erit? Veteresne poetas, an quos et praesens et postera resquat aetas?

"Iste quidem veteres inter ponetur honeste, qui vel mense brevi vel toto est iunior anno." Utor permisso, caudaeque pilos ut equinae paulatim vello unum, demo etiam unum, dum cadat elusus

TACTIC: Release bad news on Friday

If a government wants to release some bad news, they will try to do it on a Friday. That leaves time for the story to dissipate before Monday. Key financial figures may be withheld to prevent repercussions by shareholders and currency speculators. In recent cases in Britain, senior politicians were accused of withholding important news until the day a major disaster occurred. The government news was released whilst headline space was dominated by the disaster story.

TACTIC: Big headlines and "yellow journalism"

TAKE ⚠ CONTROL

Shock headlines are a diversion. Look carefully for stories that are downplayed deeper in the newspaper.

"The bigger the headline the bigger the story" was the editorial gimmick that transformed news publishing in the time of William Randolph Hearst. He was the first to evolve newspapers from information bulletins to an entertainment medium. Using banner headlines, exaggerated stories and irreverent cartoons, he shifted the emphasis of journalism and created a new style that lives on in many newspapers today.

William Randolph Hearst

William Hearst (April 29, 1863 - August 14, 1951) was an American newspaper magnate, born in San Francisco, California. In 1895, William Hearst purchased the *New York Morning Journal* and entered into a head-to-head circulation war with his former mentor, Joseph Pulitzer, owner of the *New York World*. To increase circulation both started to include articles about the Cuban Insurrection. Many stories in both newspapers greatly exaggerated their claims to make the stories more sensational. Both Hearst and Pulitzer published images of Spanish troops placing Cubans into concentration camps where they suffered and died from disease and hunger. The term yellow journalism, which was derived from the name of "The Yellow Kid" comic strip in the Journal, was used to refer to this style of sensationalized newspaper article.

From Wikipedia

Understanding the Message

PR material makes up 50% of the news content of some major newspapers. Use this quick guide to assess any news story – including the one below.

1. Try and guess the **origin** of the message?
2. Who will **benefit** from the message?
3. Does a **profit motive** affect objectivity ?
4. Are **opposing voices** included, and treated fairly?
5. What **assumptions** lie beneath the message?

SELF HELP

Crop biotechnology helps meet world food demand, safely and nutritiously

December 5, 2001... Saint Louis, Missouri... Currently, the world's population stands at more than six billion people and is growing at a rate of about 1.3 percent each year. The International Food Policy Research Institute estimates that farmers will have to produce 40 percent more grain by 2020 just to keep up with the world's rising demand for food.

Joe Russel, a farmer who grows corn and soybeans in East Central Indiana said, "Most of us in the United States have plenty of nutritious and delicious food on our table. But for nearly 800 million people around the world, starvation is an enemy that is faced everyday."

Russel is grateful for the excellent crop he recently harvested and pleased to be able to use crop biotechnology to help feed people in the United States as well as in other countries.

Biotechnology is an advancement in science that gives plant breeders an improved version of the same process that people have long used to increase crop productivity and improve the food supply.

"We are always working to improve the methods we use to grow crops on our farm, and biotechnology is one of the best tools we have to improve the quality of our environment and our food production," Russel said.

There is a limited amount of productive farmland in the world, which means people in developing countries need the ability to grow more food per acre or they will cut down trees to make room for more agricultural production. The developing world also loses vast amounts of crops to insect pests and diseases.

"Biotechnology helps create crops that are resistant to certain pests," Russel said. "By using biotechnology our yields will increase and this will help us feed people around the world."

ANSWERS: The message originated from a biotech promoter called *Tomorrowsbounty.org*, it will profit pro-biotech farmers and corporations. The central assumptions about world hunger are wrong. There is currently an oversupply of food in the world. Starvation is caused by an imbalance in the distribution of the world's food, not under-production.

TREND: Junk news

Junk news is often relied on as a "filler" to entertain bored news audiences. The result is shortened coverage of substantial issues or elimination of less "stimulating" news items. Junk news comes in the form of unpaid promotional slots for movies or TV programs and celebrity news.

BRAND NAME NEWS Britney Spears, Brad Pitt, Madonna, Robert Downey Jr.

SEX NEWS Ricky Martin's sexuality, Ellen Degeneres and Pamela Anderson's figure.

TAKE ⚠ CONTROL

Junk news is a sign of slipping editorial standards. Select papers that concentrate on matters of lasting importance.

YO YO NEWS The stock market is up or down, the crime rate is up or down, unemployment is up or down, inflation is up or down, the interest rate is up or down.

SHOW BIZ NEWS "Survivor," "Big Brother," "Who Wants To Marry a Multi-Millionaire?," "Who Wants To Be a Millionaire?"

CRAZED NEWS The latest internet craze, dot-com craze, diet craze, fashion craze, drug craze, video game craze and, of course, the always newsworthy latest crazed killer.

ANNIVERSARY NEWS Commemorating the Columbine shooting, Oklahoma bombing, Jon Benet Ramsey murder, Princess Diana accident and, the ultimate anniversary, the millennium.

SPORTS NEWS Super Bowl, Super Salaries, Super Injuries and Super Drug Problems.

POLITICAL NEWS The bi-annual political news season, when congressional candidates promise you anything to be elected, and the 2000 election that added "pregnant chads" to the political lexicon.

www.projectcensored.org

TACTIC: The Echo Chamber

"Echo chamber" is a colloquial term used to describe a group of media outlets that tend to parrot each other's uncritical reports on the views of a single source, or that otherwise rely on unquestioning repetition of official sources.

In the United States, the Republican Party uses a network of conservative foundations, coordinated by the Philanthropy Roundtable, to support an echo chamber of think tanks, industry-friendly experts and subsidized conservative media that systematically spread its messages throughout the political and media establishment. Typically, the message starts when conservative voices begin making an allegation (e.g., Democratic candidates are engaged in "hate-mongering" with regard to Bush). Columns start getting written on this theme, which spreads beyond the subsidized conservative media, eventually begins appearing in places like the *New York Times* and becomes a talking point and "accepted fact" throughout the media.

From Disinfopedia

TREND: Corporations claim the "right to lie"

A new law means companies are no longer bound by the truth in PR campaigns. While Nike was conducting a huge and expensive PR blitz to tell people that it had cleaned up its subcontractors' sweatshop labor practices, an alert consumer advocate and activist in California named Marc Kasky caught them in what he alleges are a number of specific deceptions. Nike instead chose to argue that corporations should enjoy the same "free speech" right to deceive that individual citizens have in their personal lives.

If people have the constitutionally protected right to say, "The check is in the mail," or "That looks great on you," then, Nike's reasoning goes, a corporation should have the same right to say whatever they want in their corporate PR campaigns.

TAKE CONTROL

Assess the objectivity of any third party. Are they a paid representative? Is it part of a strategic PR campaign?

Thom Hartmann - CommonDreams.org
www.unequalprotection.com

TACTIC: Third party scam used in news campaigns

In their new book *Trust Us, We're Experts: How Industry Manipulates Science and Gambles with Your Future*, Sheldon Rampton and John Stauber offer a chilling exposé on the manufacturing of "independent experts." Public relations firms and corporations have seized upon a slick new way of getting you to buy what they have to sell: they let you hear it from a neutral "third party," like a professor, a pediatrician, a soccer mom or a watchdog group. The problem is, these third parties are usually anything but neutral. They have been handpicked, cultivated and meticulously packaged to make you believe what they have to say – preferably in an "objective" format like a news show or a letter to the editor. And in some cases, they have been paid handsomely for their "opinions."

www.prwatch.org

"THE SENSIBLE ENVIRONMENTALIST"

DEAR DR. MOORE:

I'm designing a new home. Do you have any advice on building "green?"

Building green can be interpreted in different ways. Green as a measure of environmental friendliness is what I'll focus on here.

Everything we do has an impact on the environment. Designing your own home, you have an opportunity to minimize your impact through energy efficiency and the use of renewable resources.

Wood, for example, is the only major building material that is renewable. Wood products also require less energy – from extraction through manufacturing – than concrete or steel, use less fossil fuels to make, produce less water and air pollution, and result in far lower emissions of greenhouse gases. A recent study comparing buildings designed using primarily wood, steel or concrete, found the concrete design required 70 percent more energy to build and the steel design 140 percent more energy to build than the wood option.

Once your home is built, there is an even greater opportunity to save energy through efficiency and the sources of energy used to heat and cool the home, provide water, power lights and

naturally warmer in winter and cooler in summer, which translates into reduced energy consumption.

Install a high-efficiency furnace and Energy Star air conditioners and appliances, and use compact fluorescent light bulbs which consume less energy and last much longer. In some parts of the country, consumers can also choose to buy "green" energy produced by wind, hydro, and biomass (usually wood waste) The most environmentally friendly technology is the ground source heat pump that uses renewable earth energy from beneath your home to provide heat, air conditioning and hot water.

The more consumers seek out environmentally friendly designs, the more available and cost-effective they'll become. I believe a sensible environmentalist would, in building a new home, focus wherever possible on the use of wood renewable energy and energy efficiency.

Patrick Moore has been a leader of environmental movement years. A co-founder of G

Weekly "column" part of PR campaign

This is an example of a press release that has been distributed to newpapers and magazines. It is made to appear as an environmentally aware help column. In fact it is part of a sustained PR campaign by the Forest Alliance of British Columbia which represents the logging industry. Patrick Moore 's stance as an environmentalist has been publicly criticized by genuine environmentalists.

Factory journalism
How press releases are used to promote commercial interests

Forestry Industry

Doman Forest Products Ltd.
International Forest Products Ltd.
West Fraser Timber Co. Ltd.
MacMillan Bloedel Limited
Fletcher Challenge Canada Ltd.
Timber West Forest Ltd.
Ainsworth Lumber Co. Ltd.
Canfor Corporation
Crestbrook Forest Industries Ltd.
Lignum Ltd.
Northwood Pulp and Timber Limited
Pope & Talbot Limited
Riverside Forest Products Ltd.
Skeena Cellulose Inc.
Tolko Industries Ltd.
Weldwood of Canada Limited
Weyerhaeuser Canada Ltd.

Corporations finance lobby group set up by PR firm Burson-Marsteller.

Forest Alliance of British Columbia

Professional writers produce regular press releases promoting wood products

Dr Patrick Moore paid by Forest Alliance BC to pose as an objective environment commentator

PRESS RELEASE

DEAR DR. MOORE:

I'm designing a new home. Do you have any advice on building "green"?

Building green can be interpreted in different ways. Green as a measure of environmental friendliness is what I'll focus on here.

Everything we do has an impact on the environment. Designing your own home, you have an opportunity to minimize your impact through energy efficiency and the use of renewable resources.

Wood, for example, is the only major building material that is renewable. Wood products also require less energy through manufacturing to make, produce less... emissions of greenhouse... design required 70 p... 140 percent mor...

Once your home is b... energy through effic... cool the home, provi...

For example, wood is a better insulator than other construction materials—8.5 times better than concrete and 400 times better than steel. A wood-framed home that is well-insulated and sealed stays naturally warmer in winter and cooler in summer, which translates

...ory, power lights and run appliances.
...ay used to heat and

NAPS
NORTH AMERICAN PRECIS SYNDICATE

Finished article is distributed free by N.A.P.S. and included as a column in newspapers across North America.

Press release networks are replacing real journalism using packaged stories on health, lifestyle and business. Some include:
www.napsnet.com
www.prnewswire.com

CLOSE-UP
Other Media

Entertainment media including feature films, paperback fiction and the internet have increasing mass-media clout due to the cosy corporate relationships that exist within vast media empires. Product placement is not a new idea, but the extent of its use and the secretive manner in which it has been deployed has offended some consumers. The uneasy relationship between the arts and corporate interests has created disillusioned audiences who have begun to wonder which artist will be the next to sell out.

TREND: Product placement goes to the next level

Feature This promises to stay on top of every script coming through Hollywood and find opportunities to place brands in your favorite new movie. It worked powerfully for BMW when they launched their new Z3 in a James Bond flick, and who can forget Reese's Pieces, center stage in *ET*? Charlie Sheen sports a pair of Luxottica sunglasses, and the manufacturer sees sales leap to a new high. As the site boasts, "These examples demonstrate why product placement has come into its own as a marketing tool for Corporate America. Product placement has in recent years become a thoroughly professional industry. Now more widespread than ever, the business is firmly linked with broader entertainment marketing, in the form of sizeable co-promotions and joint-marketing efforts. Product placement is the practice of integrating specific products and brands into filmed entertainment. Although there is still an occasional payment by the manufacturer for "key" placements, in the majority of deals nowadays, no cash changes hands. Rather the client supplies goods or equipment for use in filming, or tosses in some extra product (food, for example) for the crew."

www.featurethis.com

PROFILE: Real time feedback taps viewer psychology

The Stanton-Lazersfeld Program Analyzer was developed at London's Tavistock Institute in the 1950s. Known as "Little Annie," the device enabled live audiences to register the intensity of their likes and dislikes of radio programs, in real time. Similar devices are now used with television shows to assess how particular characters or situations produced the desired feelings in the target audience. Telemarketing presenters use feedback during live television ads to fine-tune their gestures and script and voice volume based on the number of order calls being registered.

members.tripod.com/~american_almanac/polls.htm

TREND: Journalists sneak promotion into column

Ads in the form of what appear to be journalistic articles formed part of a new "feature by Sony" campaign. The articles were written by freelance writers and are designed to appear as editorial content on popular web sites. The pieces are geared toward Sony's specific consumer segments to show how consumers can integrate technology into their lives. While this appeared tasteful, it contravened ethical standards that require such articles to be labeled as advertorials.

CASE STUDY: Brands in song lyrics

There were 82 different brands mentioned in the Billboard Top 20 songs in 2003. *The Jump Off* by Lil' Kim featured 14 different brand names in a single song. Other artists have used this method as a back door tactic to attract sponsorship.

Recording artist Nelly featured Nike's Air Force Ones in his song – which resulted in the release of his own signature Nelly Nike shoe. Run-DMC wrote a song called "My Adidas" which led to a sponsorship deal worth $1.5 million. These lines by Busta Rhymes resulted in a major upsurge in the sale of Courvoisier Cognac:

But if your man baby sittin, then what you gon' say
(What we gon' tell 'em man?)
We gon' tell that nigga (Pass the Courvoisier)
We gon' tell that brotha (Pass the Courvoisier)
Everybody sing it now (Pass the Courvoisier)
Everybody sing it now (Pass the Courvoisier)

Rapper 50 Cent is the artist most likely to mention brands in his songs. He did it thirty-one times within one year.

The brands mentioned most often in the Billboard Top 20 during 2003 were: Mercedes (112 mentions), Lexus (48 mentions), Gucci (47 mentions), Cadillac (46 mentions), Burberry (42 mentions), Prada (39 mentions), Cristal (37 mentions), Hennessy (35 mentions), Lamborghini (34 mentions) and Chevrolet (33 mentions).

Source: American Brandstand at www.AgendaInc.com

CASE STUDY: Big brands woven into fiction

For years, books were one of the few mediums free from huckstering. But publishers have recently put product placements in books, especially those targeted at children. And so there are now children's books touting many brands of junk food, including Fruit Loops, M & M's, Reese's Pieces, Skittles, Hershey's chocolates and Oreo cookies. Product placement is coming to more adult works, too. Fay Weldon's new work, featuring the Bulgari jewelry company, is an advertisement, not a novel.

www.commercialalert.org

RESEARCH

Fay Weldon wrote a book called

The Bulgari Connection

'A glorious romp of love, lust, greed and power.'
The Times

THE BVLGARI CONNECTION

FAY WELDON

commissioned by the Italian jewelry firm of that name. Her contract required that she use the name of the company at least twelve times. It included strategically placed sales snippets throughout.

"...sleek modern piece, a necklace, stripes of white and yellow gold, but encasing three ancient coins, the mount flowing the irregular contours of thin, worn bronze..."

CLOSE-UP

Public Relations

The most successful public relations campaigns aim to change public perception without our awareness of the campaign.

They are regularly conducted by governments, institutions and countries that are endeavoring to change their public image, restore their reputation or manipulate public opinion. When these firms have aided dictatorships, dishonest politicians and corrupt industries, the results have led to environmental catastrophes, human rights violations and war.

"We are dominated by the relatively small number of persons who understand the mental processes and social patterns of the masses. It is they who pull the wires that control the public mind."

Edward Bernays

Public relations (PR) is a communications strategy aiming to influence specific publics using writing, marketing, advertising, publicity, promotions, and special events. Some public relations specialists work as full-time employees of companies, politicians, nonprofit organizations or governments; while others work for PR agencies that contract their services to clients (usually corporations, wealthy individuals or other special interests) who pay for their expertise at keeping them in or out of the spotlight, whichever is necessary.

Public relations tactics

Corporations are increasingly manipulative in the way that they present information via Front Groups, and information media. PR Watch is a quarterly publication of the Center for Media & Democracy. PRs have often engaged in deliberate deception on their clients' behalf and have developed a deeply unhealthy relationship with the "free press."

RESEARCH

Edward Bernays
The father of public relations

Edward Bernays (November 22, 1891 - March 9, 1995). Born in Vienna, Bernays was a nephew of Sigmund Freud, the father of psychoanalysis. Bernays also pioneered the PR industry's use of psychology and other social sciences to design its public persuasion campaigns. He called this scientific technique of opinion molding the "engineering of consent."

In *Propaganda*, his most important book, Bernays argued that the scientific manipulation of public opinion was necessary to overcome chaos and conflict in society.

"The conscious and intelligent manipulation of the organized habits and opinions of the masses is an important element in democratic society. Those who manipulate this unseen mechanism of society constitute an invisible government which is the true ruling power of our country. ... We are governed, our minds are molded, our tastes formed, our ideas suggested, largely by men we have never heard of. This is a logical result of the way in which our democratic society is organized. Vast numbers of human beings must cooperate in this manner if they are to live together as a smoothly functioning society. ... In almost every act of our daily lives, whether in the sphere of politics or business, in our social conduct or our ethical thinking, we are dominated by the relatively small number of persons... who understand the mental processes and social patterns of the masses. It is they who pull the wires which control the public mind."

Furthermore, by giving vested interests the opportunity to deliberately obfuscate, deceive and derail public debate on key issues the public relations industry reduces society's capacity to respond effectively to key social, environmental and political challenges.

www.prwatch.org

CASE STUDY: Wartime propaganda

In October 2003, US Soldiers stationed in Iraq sent a flood of "letters to the editor" to their hometown newspapers claiming rapid progress in the restoration of law and order in Iraq. The only problem was that all of the "letters" were the same word for word. Previously this would have gone unnoticed, but modern Internet searching technology picked it up very quickly. Although a military officer reportedly instigated the campaign, the Pentagon distanced itself from the embarrassing initiative – which coincided with a coordinated public relations campaign undertaken by the White House to bolster domestic support for Operation Iraqi Freedom.

CASE STUDY: Office of Strategic Influence

The Office of Strategic Influence, or OSI, was planned as a center for the creation of U.S. propaganda materials, for the stated purpose of misleading enemy forces or their civilian populations for "Operation Enduring Freedom" in 2001. It may surprise some that propaganda is a part of a modern wartime strategy, but despite a public outcry which shut it down, it resurfaced under another name.

"And then there was the Office of Strategic Influence. [...] I went down that next day and said fine, if you want to savage this thing fine I'll give you the corpse. There's the name. You can have the name, but I'm gonna keep doing every single thing that needs to be done and I have." - **Secretary of Defense Donald Rumsfeld, 2002-11-18 [2], from Wikipedia**

Retired U.S. Air Force Colonel Sam Gardiner, who has taught strategy and military operations at the National War College, produced an analysis which suggests that the White House and Pentagon made up or distorted more than 50 news stories related to the war in Iraq, including:

- Chemical weapons in Drones
- Nuclear materials from Niger
- Aluminum tubes
- Nuclear weapons development

How to Engineer Public Opinion

Corporate Message
Determine how the public perception needs to be changed - to meet strategic goals of corporation or government.

Focus Group
Sift for thought patterns which can be exploited and manipulated.

Targeted Message
Reframe the issue using "symbols" and "stories" to influence thought patterns.

Opinion Polls
Measured for effectiveness of message.

Front Group

News Media

Paid Expert

General Public
Final targeted message absorbed, processed and discussed by the public, beginning a process of changed perceptions, beliefs and behaviors.

Opinion Engineer's Tool Kit

#1: Focus Groups

Focus groups are often used in tandem with opinion polls, in which PR specialists survey a representative sample of their "target population" and ask each member of the sample an identical set of questions. When a large enough sample is queried, the pollster can claim to have "scientifically measured" the current state of opinion with regard to those questions.

Rather than interviewing a large sample using standardized questions, the researcher selects a small group of individuals and leads them through open-ended interrogations aimed at eliciting not only which answer they choose but why they choose it. If you prefer Pepsi, for example, the focus group might ask if your preference is based on the color of the cans or their feelings about Britney Spears. By understanding underlying constellations of attitudes and perceptions, marketers hope to be able to better "focus" their message.

From Disinfopedia, the encyclopedia of propaganda

#2: Doublespeak

Clever substitution of words can change the public response to an emotional issue. Word association techniques aim to surround the issue with favorable associations to distract from the facts.

William Lutz, a professor at Rutgers University, has written several books about doublespeak, which examines ways that jargon has polluted the public mindspace with phrases designed to obscure the meaning of plain English.

In 1992, the International Food Information Council hired Dr. G. Clotaire Rapaille, a Jungian psychoanalyst, to advise them on ways to win public support for GM foods. Rapaille provided a list of "words to use" and "words to lose" when talking about the topic. The "words to use" included terms such as beauty, bounty, children, choices, cross-breeding, diversity, earth, farmer, flowers, fruits, future generations, hard work, heritage, improved, organic, purity, quality, soil, tradition and wholesome. "Words to lose" included: biotechnology, chemical, DNA, economic, experiments, industry, laboratory, machines, manipulate, money, pesticides, profit, radiation, safety and scientists.

Examples:

aerial ordnance = bombs

biosolids = sewage sludge

defense = war

Opinion Engineer's Tool Kit

downsize = lay off employees

ethnic cleansing = genocide

liberate = invade

neutralize = kill

pre-hostility = peace

spin = lie

take down = kill

From Disinfopedia

#3: Front Groups

A front group is an organization that purports to represent one agenda while in reality it serves some other party or interest whose sponsorship is hidden or rarely mentioned. For example, the Center for Consumer Freedom (CCF) claims that its mission is to defend the rights of consumers to choose to eat, drink and smoke as they please. In reality, CCF is a front group for the tobacco, restaurant and alcoholic beverage industries, which provide all of its funding.

#4: Paid Experts

The propaganda industry uses two types of industry-friendly experts: (1) people who work behind the scenes as expert advisors, using psychology and other specialized expertise to design PR and advertising campaigns, and (2) experts for the public stage, who (a) pretend to speak as disinterested, knowledgeable authorities with regard to some public issue, or (b) being professionally incompetent, actually serve some special interest.

Many experts in this second category receive funding or other immediate personal reward for acting as special interest spokespersons. For example, Elizabeth Whelan of the American Council on Science and Health routinely dismisses health risks and environmental harm from pesticides and other toxic chemicals, while earning a six-figure annual salary that is largely funded by the chemical industry and agribusiness. Many experts for hire, such as Steven Milloy, flatly refuse to discuss where they get their funding, and the front groups and think tanks that employ them are not required to disclose their funding sources.

From Disinfopedia

Opinion Engineer's Tool Kit

#5: Opinion Polls

Opinion Polls do more than present opinions. They are also used as a medium for social manipulation. When people read the results of a poll in the newspaper, they often use it as a guide for developing their own opinion. By using deceptive question techniques, some pollsters engineer results to present a predetermined message.

TAKE CONTROL

Value your individuality. Don't let the results of opinion polls change you.

"Polls prove that people are stupid," said Hal Becker, who headed the Connecticut-based Futures Group, an outfit which specialized in sophisticated polling of the U.S. and other national populations.

"If you want an American to believe something, then all you have to do is get a poll taken that says it is so (and believe me, that is an easy thing to do, if you know how), and then get it publicized. You can tell somebody the Moon is made of green cheese – if the poll numbers say it is so, then the jerk reading them or watching them on the boob tube will believe it. Guaranteed."

Source: The American Almanac, May 1997

#6: Transfer Technique

"Transfer is a device by which the propagandist carries over the authority, sanction, and prestige of something we respect and revere to something he would have us accept," explained the now-defunct Institute for Propaganda Analysis in its 1938 analysis of this common rhetorical technique. "For example, most of us respect and revere our church and our nation. If the propagandist succeeds in getting church or nation to approve a campaign in behalf of some program, he thereby transfers its authority, sanction, and prestige to that program. Thus, we may accept something which otherwise we might reject.

TAKE CONTROL

Be wary of politicians or companies overusing patriotism. Examine why such emotional appeals are being used in the place of reason.

"In the Transfer device, symbols are constantly used. The cross represents the Christian Church. The flag represents the nation. Cartoons like Uncle Sam represent a consensus of public opinion. Those symbols stir emotions. At their very sight, with the speed of thought, is aroused the whole complex of feelings we have with respect to church or nation."

From Disinfopedia

Opinion Engineer's Tool Kit

#7: PR Consultants

Public Relations firms handle strategic communications for large corporations, organizations and governments. They are a major force in the world of corporate communications. These are the revenues for the top five of 2001:

1 Weber Shandwick Worldwide $426,572,018
2 Fleishman-Hillard Inc. $345,098,241
3 Hill and Knowlton, Inc. $325,119,000
4 Incepta (Citigate) $266,018,371
5 Burson Marsteller $259,112,000

UK based researcher Corporate Watch has uncovered a darker side to the PR industry, "There is a considerable body of evidence emerging to suggest that modern public relations practices are having a very significant deleterious impact on the democratic process... PRs have often engaged in deliberate deception on their clients' behalf and have developed a deeply unhealthy relationship with the 'free press.' Furthermore, by giving vested interests the opportunity to deliberately obfuscate, deceive, and derail public debate on key issues the public relations industry reduces society's capacity to respond effectively to key social, environmental and political challenges."

www.corporatewatch.org.uk

CASE STUDY: Biotech firms target teenagers

Monsanto Germany, Novartis Germany and AgrEvo targeted German teenagers in a 1998 issue of the teen magazine *Bravo Girly*, which carried a pullout supplement ("Gen Food") that sought to make GE cool. Features of the supplement included:

• Teen interviews with the genetic engineer Hans Olaf Warning ("He doesn't look like Frankenstein. He seems like a really good guy.")

• A visit to 17 year-old Lisa's farm, where her father is growing GE crops (during which time a young visitor, Sven, falls in love with Lisa).

TAKE ⚠ **CONTROL**

Large corporations can afford major communications campaigns. Always weigh their claims and assumptions by consulting independent researchers.

• A quiz to test your knowledge of genetic engineering (and win wrist watches or packets of genetic biscuits).

• A question/answer forum: teen questions on the benefits and safety of genetic engineering are answered by an unidentified columnist. Readers with further questions could call a hotline.

Teen Zines provide a particularly malleable audience for GE promotion: the readership is typically a narrow social group (predominantly teenagers and below) with limited exposure to non-establishment political views or analysis. There is little or no scope for peer opposition to genetic engineering in such a forum, so a pro-GE analysis is likely to go unchallenged.

Confessions of a spin doctor

"Business is booming. We outnumber journalists and the gap is increasing. The reason is simple: public relations works.

"We write stories that our clients want us to write, send them to newspapers, magazines or TV stations and journalists write their stories using our information. Often they'll get another perspective on the topic by contacting another source and call that 'balanced reporting.'

"Sometimes they won't – we really liked it when that happened. It meant that our message wasn't diluted by an opposing opinion. If we were lucky, the journalists we contacted would be lazy or overworked. That way they wouldn't have the time or energy to come up with their own story angles, quotes or research, and they'd just use ours – our quotes, our research, our priorities... Don't believe it when you read a story about heart disease and the statistics they use come from a pharmaceutical company – even if they quote a doctor (they're on the payroll too)."

www.prwatch.org

CASE STUDY: The Rendon Group

The Rendon Group is a secretive public relations firm that has assisted a number of U.S. military interventions in nations including Argentina, Colombia, Haiti, Iraq, Kosovo, Panama and Zimbabwe. Rendon's activities including organizing the Iraqi National Congress, a PR front group designed to foment the overthrow of Iraqi dictator Saddam Hussein.

In a 1998 speech to the National Security Conference (NSC), president John W. Rendon, Jr. described himself as "an information warrior, and a perception manager. This is probably best described in the words of Hunter S. Thompson, when he wrote 'When things turn weird, the weird turn pro.'"

TAKE ⚠ **CONTROL**
Familiarize yourself with the methods and history of the major PR firms. Note their client lists and the nature of their projects.

"Through its network of international offices and strategic alliances," the Rendon Group web site boasted in 2002, "the company has provided communications services to clients in more than 78 countries, and maintains contact with government officials, decision-makers, and news media around the globe."

From Wikipedia

CASE STUDY: Burson-Marsteller

The Burson-Marsteller website indicates the extent of their influence on behalf of their clients: "Burson-Marsteller is the world's leading public affairs network. Operating at the intersection where business concerns often collide with public policy issues, we help clients navigate difficult challenges that—if left unchecked—could undermine growth, reduce market share or damage an institution's reputation. In virtually every major market and capital in the world, we have senior professionals who are experts in influencing debates surrounding contentious legislative and regulatory issues."

www.bm.com

How to Detect Propaganda

This is a guide circulated before the Second World War to help citizens decipher loaded political messages. In modern times the techniques remain the same, though our Western governments use them in more sophisticated ways in political addresses and government advertising campaigns where they regularly employ the Transfer device and the Testimonial.

1. THE NAME CALLING DEVICE

"Name Calling" is a device to make us form a judgment without examining the evidence on which it should be based. Here the propagandist appeals to our hate and fear. He does this by giving "bad names" to those individuals, groups, nations, races, policies, practices, beliefs, and ideals which he would have us condemn and reject.

2. THE GLITTERING GENERALITIES DEVICE

"Glittering Generalities" is a device by which the propagandist identifies his program with virtue by use of "virtue words." Here he appeals to our emotions of love, generosity, and brotherhood. He uses words like truth, freedom, honor, liberty, social justice, public service, the right to work, loyalty, progress, democracy, the American way, Constitution-defender. These words suggest shining ideals. All persons of good will believe in these ideals. Hence the propagandist, by identifying his individual group, nation, race, policy, practice, or belief with such ideals, seeks to win us to his cause. As Name Calling is a device to make us form a judgment to reject and condemn without examining the evidence, Glittering Generalities is a device to make us accept and approve without examining the evidence.

3. THE TRANSFER DEVICE

"Transfer" is a device by which the propagandist carries over the authority, sanction, and prestige of something we respect and revere to something he would have us accept. For example, most of us respect and revere our church and our nation. If the propagandist succeeds in getting church or nation to approve a campaign in behalf of some program, he thereby transfers its authority, sanction, and prestige to that program. Thus we may accept something which otherwise we might reject...In the Transfer device, symbols are constantly used. The cross represents the Christian Church. The flag represents the nation. Cartoons like Uncle Sam represent a consensus of public opinion.

4. THE TESTIMONIAL DEVICE

The "Testimonial" is a device to make us accept anything from a patent medicine or a cigarette to a program of national policy. In this device the propagandist makes use of testimonials. "When I feel tired, I smoke a Camel and get the grandest 'lift.'" "We believe the John L. Lewis plan of labor organization is splendid; C.I.O. should be supported." This device works in reverse also; counter-testimonials may be employed.

5. THE PLAIN FOLKS DEVICE

"Plain Folks" is a device used by politicians, labor leaders, businessmen, and even by ministers and educators to win our confidence by appearing to be people like ourselves-"just plain folks among the neighbors." In election years especially do candidates show their devotion to little children and the common, homey things of life.

6. THE CARD STACKING DEVICE

"Card Stacking" is a device in which the propagandist employs all the arts of deception to win our support for himself, his group, nation, race, policy, practice, belief, or ideal. He stacks the cards against the truth. He uses under-emphasis and over-emphasis to dodge issues and evade facts. He resorts to lies, censorship, and distortion. He omits facts. He offers false testimony. He creates a smoke screen of clamor by raising a new issue when he wants an embarrassing matter forgotten. He draws a red herring across the trail to confuse and divert those in quest of facts he does not want revealed. He makes the unreal appear real and the real appear unreal. He lets half-truth masquerade as truth. By the Card Stacking device, a mediocre candidate, through the buildup, is made to appear an intellectual titan; an ordinary prize fighter; a probable world champion; a worthless patent medicine, a beneficent cure. By means of this device propagandists would convince us that a ruthless war of aggression is a crusade for righteousness.

7. THE BAND WAGON DEVICE

The "Band Wagon" is a device to make us follow the crowd, to accept the propagandist's program en masse. Here his theme is: "Everybody's doing it." His techniques range from those of medicine show to dramatic spectacle. He hires a hall, fills a great stadium, marches a million men in parade. He employs symbols, colors, music, movement, all the dramatic arts. He appeals to the desire, common to most of us, to "follow the crowd." Because he wants us to follow the crowd" in masses, he directs his appeal to groups held together by common ties of nationality, religion, race environment, sex, vocation. Thus propagandists campaigning for or against a program will appeal to us as Catholics, Protestants, or Jews; as members of the Nordic race or as Negroes; as farmers or as school teachers; as housewives or as miners. All the artifices of flattery are used to harness the fears and hatreds, prejudices, and biases, convictions and ideals common to the group; thus emotion is made to push and pull the group on to the Band Wagon.

CLOSE-UP

Schools

As corporations become more desperate to develop brand loyalty, some have targeted young children.

Apart from being a market themselves, children influence their parents' spending across the board. For schools under financial pressure, the temptation of corporate handouts is too great.

TREND: Selling out our schools

Most people consider our public schools to be hallowed ground, where young Americans of various religions, races, and social strata collectively learn the tools of citizenship. Yet multinational corporations now view our children's schools as convenient locations for the dissemination of propaganda, debunking of environmental concerns and as the tip of an unimaginably profitable marketing iceberg. The stakes are incredibly high.

CASE STUDY: Cover Concepts

A company has found yet another space for companies to leave their mark on impressionable minds. "Cover Concepts offers a medium which penetrates an almost advertising-free environment – the public school," the company explains in its promotional material. School children amount to "a captive audience," the brochures add.

Despite such pitches, the company has largely sidestepped controversy. Its marketing hasn't inspired the sort of furor that erupted over K-III Communications Corp.'s Channel One classroom newscasts containing commercials. For one thing, Cover Concepts doesn't pester reluctant schools, according to Mr. Yanoff, the 32-year-old chief executive. And, in fact, fewer than 1% refuse. "It's funny. We aren't nearly as controversial, mainly because we aren't broadcasting," he says.

www.stayfreemagazine.org/archives/13/manipulated.html

CASE STUDY: Channel One

"Would you want your children to see propaganda that glorifies reckless driving or that reinforces the poor body image of teenage girls? That's exactly the kind of thing schoolkids are watching on Channel One, a so-called educational broadcast piped into classrooms across the country. Whether your main concern is quality of education, the role of corporations in our culture, or the commercial values children are exposed to, there is great reason to be concerned about Channel One. In essence, Channel One is run by a marketing company that uses the schools to deliver advertising to youngsters. Each school day, work comes to a halt in classrooms across the nation as teachers turn on a TV show made up of two minutes of commercials and 10 minutes of 'news.'" –Ralph Nader

www.nader.org/interest/051299.html

Why corporations are targeting schools

- According to recent marketing industry studies, a person's "brand loyalty" may begin as early as age two.

- Experts say a lifetime customer may be worth $100,000 to a retailer, making effective "cradle to grave" strategies extremely valuable.

- The teen audience of Channel One is 50 times the MTV teen audience.

- Children's spending has roughly doubled every ten years for the past three decades.

- In 1997, kids influenced $188 billion of their parents' purchases.

- In 1997, kids aged 4-12 spent $23.4 billion.

- It's estimated the average child sees between 20,000-40,000 commercials every year.

- At six months of age, babies are forming mental images of corporate logos and mascots.

www.newdream.org

Channel One

charges $200,000 for 30 seconds of air time to companies such as Nike, Nintendo, Pepsi and Burger King.

"The news is not the point of Channel One. It is no more than filler ... meant primarily to get us ready for the ads... Channel One teaches students six messages: 'Watch.' 'Don't Think.' 'Let Us Fix It.' 'Eat Now.' 'You're Ugly.' and 'Just Say Yes.'"

Mark Crispin Miller, Professor of Culture and Communication, New York University. His study of Channel One was entitled: "How to Be Stupid: The Teachings of Channel One," January 27, 1997

Channel One protest sites:
www.obligation.org
www.adbusters.org

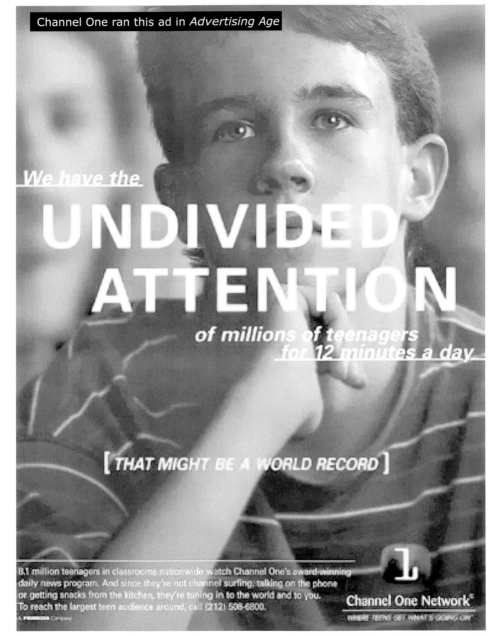

Channel One ran this ad in *Advertising Age*

We have the

UNDIVIDED ATTENTION

*of millions of teenagers
for 12 minutes a day*

[*THAT MIGHT BE A WORLD RECORD*]

8.1 million teenagers in classrooms nationwide watch Channel One's award-winning
daily news program. And since they're not channel surfing, talking on the phone
or getting snacks from the kitchen, they're tuning in to the world and to you.
To reach the largest teen audience around, call (212) 508-6800.

A PRIMEDIA Company

Channel One Network®
WHERE TEENS GET WHAT'S GOING ON

The Personal Zone

"Word of mouth is one of the oldest communications tools. But there's a nice irony here: The more sophisticated technology becomes, the more marketers focus on the human jaw, and how to put it in motion."

AD AGE

We Know What You Want
Chapter 4: **The Personal Zone**

Strong families, friendships and communities are vital to our sense of personal security. But for many companies and cults, these relationships are just another medium to be exploited.

Buzz terms like "network marketing" and "viral marketing" legitimize making money from your friends. For those desperate to extend their market, friends and family are convenient targets.

Other companies have created new media to invade your personal space in public areas of the neighborhood or city streets, and via the telephone.

- **Network marketing**
- **Cult recruitment**
- **Viral marketing**
- **Telemarketing**
- **Buzz agents**

CLOSE-UP

Friendships

There are new ways to infiltrate personal friendships in order to introduce word-of-mouth buzz on an idea or product.

The emerging science of memetics has created a new branch of advertising that specifically aims to construct messages that will be passed rapidly from person to person. Memetics studies the characteristics of contagious ideas - everything from fads, religions and habits, to slogans and logos. Businesses have used memetics to create buzz marketing and viral marketing. Now they can use your relationships to peddle their products.

Others have applied memetics to market research, identifying segments of the population who will be ideal carriers for certain ideas.

Multi-level marketers have used a crude form of memetics to promote health food household products. A variation of the pyramid scheme, known as network marketing, has turned the social fabric into a distribution channel.

TREND: Promotion from person to person

It may be the oldest form of advertising but it is getting extra attention from today's experts. Word-of-mouth is now recognized as the most powerful form of publicity. As trust in advertising declines, marketers are looking for ways to buy word-of-mouth advertising from those who are willing to sell their conversations. For the cost of a television spot, a company can buy hundreds of buzz agents, who agree to sneak their message into the conversation. Using the science of memetics, the message can be fine-tuned to travel further.

THEORY: Memetics

Memetics is the study of how ideas pass from from one person to another across a culture. The term was coined by Richard Dawkins in his controversial book *The Selfish Gene*. It proposed that some ideas were like viruses that can be transmitted from person to person and rapidly "infect" large populations. Memes can represent parts of ideas, languages, tunes, designs, moral and esthetic values, skills, and anything else that is commonly learned and passed on to others as a unit. The study of memes is called memetics.

> **TAKE ⚠ CONTROL**
>
> **Build awareness about buzz marketing.** As more people learn how it works, they recognize it, and prevent unethical practices.

TREND: Using memetics to turn friends into sales reps

Certain slogans and products have an uncanny way of catching on and becoming a global phenomenon. "Just do it," *Pokemon*, "Axis of Evil," "Wazzup." Catchy ideas used to spread by accident, but now it's a science. Memetics practitioners, known as Buzz Marketers, are now learning how to construct messages or merchandise that will turn into a social phenomenon. Using word association techniques, complex algorithms and social research, it is possible to "plant" an idea that becomes a hot topic of conversation – replacing the use of mass media.

TACTIC: Buzz marketing creates word-of-mouth epidemics

When someone you know casually mentions a new soft drink or CD, you pay attention, because an authentic endorsement conveys trust and honesty. Buzz marketers have developed ways to stimulate these casual endorsements and engineer a wave of mouth-to-mouth publicity. Buzz agents are paid to get the word out to friends and acquaintances they meet throughout the day. By posing as a fanatic for a new product they can make dozens of promotional contacts per day. Using a team of agents, it is possible to cover a strategic proportion of a target market, which in turn creates a wave effect across a community.

One Buzz agent shares her technique: "Called my sister, on my dinner break, tonight. Talked about various things including what we want for Christmas. I

One in ten tells the other nine what to do.

"Influentials"

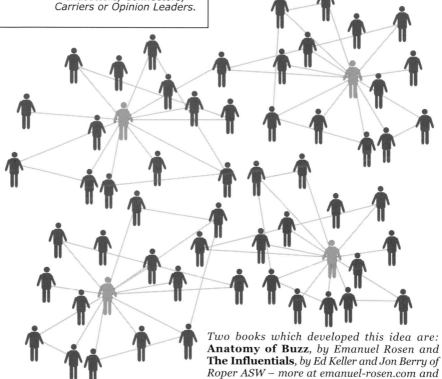

These people may be from all walks of life - hairdressers, carpenters, managers - and you meet some every day. The difference is when this 10 per cent talk, their opinions have a wide influence. *Also known as Trendsetters, Connectors, Carriers or Opinion Leaders.*

Influentials may look like ordinary people, but the word-of-mouth from this 10% has a powerful influence. Trend trackers and viral marketers have determined that these people unknowingly control political trends, fashion and the economy.

Two books which developed this idea are: **Anatomy of Buzz**, *by Emanuel Rosen and* **The Influentials**, *by Ed Keller and Jon Berry of Roper ASW – more at emanuel-rosen.com and roperasw.com*

Engineering word-of-mouth.

Marketers have realized that word-of-mouth has the biggest influence over consumer decisions. By targeting Influentials with giveaways and new products, they can create a "viral" impact that spreads across a community. This is called product seeding. Many companies are pouring all their resources into locating these people and turning them into an underground sales force.

By giving a *Ford Focus* to 120 Influentials for six months. Ford was able to create a high impact across five major cities.

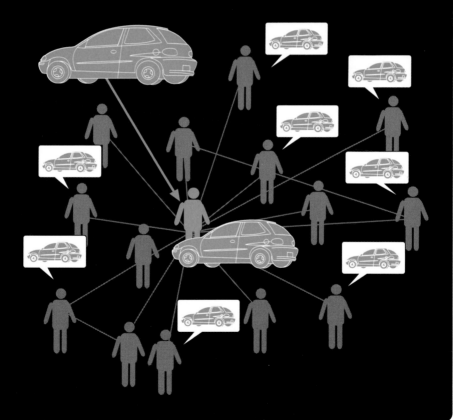

couldn't resist throwing in a little "Bzz": it was almost too easy. I told her that Wayne, her boyfriend, would love a copy of this new book I was reading... I'm an artist and always trying new and zany products... so I told her that it was kind of a strange book, but nothing so over the top that Wayne wouldn't like it. (from BzzAgent.com)

Another "Bzz" agent publicized on the above website took the opportunity to "sell" his friend on a new release book: "So, we get home from a club around 3am and we mix up some more drinks turn on my friends Nintendo 64 to have a little drunken Mario Cart competition... anyways, amidst the game, I mention that I've heard of this really cool program called G4 that I heard about from a friend of mine (wink, wink)... Me and my friend went out for coffee this afternoon and we were talking about what we were planning to get people for Xmas. She told me that she wanted to get something for her massage therapist but she couldn't really think of anything. I asked her what he's like and she told me he's very into yoga and natural remedies: he's this older hippie type. and then told her that 'my roommate' (wink, wink) bought this phat book (The Art of Shen Ku) that would be perfect."

Making the Buzz more contagious

Two Harvard University psychologists – Gordon W. Allport and Leo Postman – studied wartime rumors and came up with a mathematical formula that described the way an idea passes from person to person. They published their findings in a 1947 book, *The Psychology of Rumor*. This formula may explain how some messages spread so rapidly. It reveals how new information can be contagious without necessarily being true.

$$\mathbf{R} = \mathbf{i} \times \mathbf{a}$$

Reach = importance x ambiguity

'R'　is the **reach** of the message

'i'　is the **importance** of the message (will this effect me or enhance my life?)

'a'　is the level of **ambiguity** surrounding the message (is it new or unusual?)

THEORY: One in ten of your friends is an "Influential"

In every society a handful of people lead the opinions of those around them. Some "Influentials" are visible, like politicians or CEOs, but others are regular people who have influence due to their personality or their communication style. Several books, including *The Influentials*, *The Tipping Point* and *Anatomy of Buzz* have shown the potential of memetics to take market research to a new level. Influentials, or Opinion Leaders, are now being successfully targeted to become conscious or unconscious agents for their message. Researching firm Roper ASW claims "Influentials are so networked, they are the first to know about many things, and they in turn spread the word to others. They are the major generators of word-of-mouth recommendations in our society."

www.roperasw.com

> **TAKE ⚠ CONTROL**
>
> **Can you recognize the influentials in your community?** Learn to recognize the way they impact the opinions of those around them. Don't be afraid to disagree with them.

CASE STUDY: Pox campaign

When launching its wireless electronic game "Pox," Hasbro did extensive social research. By asking thousands of boys which of their friends they thought was the "coolest," they identified a group of core influentials. They offered cash incentives to the "coolest" boys to take the devices and show them to their friends. By employing a small percentage of key opinion leaders, they were able to influence a hard-to-reach group from the inside out.

CASE STUDY: Neighborhood moms become hot dog promoters

ConAgra Foods searched 12 cities for 250 PTA presidents, community leaders to join "mom squads" to promote "Hebrew National" hot-dogs. The ladies hosted backyard barbeques and handed out discount coupons. By using respected community representatives they attracted credibility to the brand and stimulated sales.

How to Win Friends and Influence People

Dale Carnegie's popular 1936 book led the way in legitimizing manipulation in interpersonal communication. It offered techniques about how to "Arouse in the other person an eager want," "Encourage others to talk about themselves," "Get the other person saying 'yes, yes' immediately," "Appeal to the nobler motives," "Change People Without Giving Offense," "Call attention to people's mistakes indirectly" and "Make the other person happy about doing the thing you suggest."

> **TAKE ⚠ CONTROL**
>
> **If you belong to a network marketing group - value your friends by not marketing to them.** Wait until they make a request before offering information or products.

Invitations to join multi-level marketing

Many people get tricked into joining a network marketing company because of social obligation. Victims are contacted by an old friend or a new friend who wants to meet without mentioning their intention to sign you up to buy into a business. The get-together begins and soon the person starts a sales pitch which is a scripted conversation. Due to the attraction of making money, or the wish to prevent embarrasment, many express interest. Little do they know that they are now under deeper obligation. To back out at this stage may offend and harm the relationship. Many begin on this path, often handing over substantial sums of money with no return.

"Drop Out Rate" of MLM programs

The "Drop Out Rate" of MLM programs is enormous – 98% will drop out immediately, meaning that only 2% will continue with the program over a long period of time. Plenty of money can be made from failing members before they quit - with some spending thousands of dollars on training materials and membership fees before giving up.

Relationships that were seriously damaged through involvement in a well known multilevel marketing (MLM) organization

"I have personally witnessed [MLM] destroy a family. They have turned the distributors against those living in their house. This business, which promotes family and working [MLM] in your spare time, giving you the time to be with your family, pulls this distributor away from their family every single weekend for a convention here or there – with no regard to their real family or activities within. They won't make a 5 hr drive to visit a son or daughter, but a 36 hour drive to an 8 hour convention and then [a] return 36 hr drive – no problem."

– Anonymous

"I am a former [MLM] distributor here in (Mid-west)... I signed up in 1997 and was constantly bothered to attend opens, seminars, conventions and to get the tapes and books. My upline was my best friend's father that I had known for years. He constantly berated me for not attending conventions saying that it will set me back another 3 months. I was told to skip a wedding in my family and attend that weekend's convention. One of my good friends signed up under me and was constantly bothered to get on the system. I was told to pester him and get him on it. I have no solid proof that tapes were overcharged. However I can tell you that the price of them was $6.60 and that opens

were $5 and that seminars were $15. I never attended a convention but every time one came up I was constantly bothered to do so."

– Anonymous

"I too have been duped by the [MLM] business. I spent three years and $20,000 trying to build a distributorship. I was tricked in believing that I could also build a successful, wealthy business while all the time I was spending myself into debt, alienating myself from my family and my friends and working myself to a frazzle. My upline pressured me into driving miles and miles thinking I was helping my business when in reality, I was making them more and more money." **–Anonymous**

"My husband has been involved with [MLM] 17 years. He has never made a dime. While he has always made some money from [MLM] we have turned around and spent it all on the [MLM] motivational materials and meetings. It becomes an addiction – every bit as much as alcohol or drugs can be an addiction. While some may say that the consequences are not as bad it is this addiction that has come to control every aspect of our lives, and the results are psychologically damaging." **– Anonymous**

EXCERPT: Pyramids and the Ponzi effect

"Multilevel marketing businesses degenerate into outright pyramid schemes as the products or benefits being offered become less and less tangible. Although a majority of the money is made in membership fees and commissions, most MLMs have a genuine product to sell, even if it's at a noncompetitive price. Less outwardly reputable, fly-by-night multilevel marketing schemes sell nothing more than membership in a get-rich scenario. These Ponzis only promise that if you pay money to the person at the top of the pyramid, eventually you will be at the top of the pyramid yourself, and then other people will send you some money, too.

The transparently greed-oriented Ponzi scheme gets its name from Charles Ponzi, an Italian immigrant and successful Boston investment broker who sought to capitalize on the simple principle of geometric progression. In 1920, he set up an investment scheme that promised fifty percent profit in forty-five days for all who invested in his foreign postal coupons. He was able to fulfill his wild guarantees by paying off early investors with the cash he collected from growing hordes of newcomers. He collected more than $9,500,000 in this manner. Within six months, however, Ponzi had run out of new investors from whom he could get the money to pay off those whose coupons had matured. Thousands of people lost their life savings, and Ponzi was sent to prison. His name was forever equated with the pyramid investment game."

TAKE ⚠ CONTROL

If you are interested in a network marketing opportunity, look over these questions. Assess the way the opportunity might affect your relationships and your credibility.

- Coercion

Tests for evaluating a network marketing "opportunity"

1. THE OPPORTUNITY TEST

Were you approached primarily on the basis of the actual value and need for the products – or for the "opportunity?" If the latter, the program may actually be a pyramid device for enriching the company and a small group of upline distributors.

Another red flag to look for is promoters who talk of "getting in on the ground floor" or "riding the wave" of opportunity. Usually, the bulk of the income in these cases is already locked in by the founding distributors in the pyramidal hierarchy.

2. THE INCOME DISCLOSURE TEST

If an MLM recruiter touts huge income figures of top distributors, request that the company disclose average payout to distributors by percentiles (highest 1%, second highest 1%, and so on to the lowest 1%), so that you can determine your chances of success. Ask for **net payout (after subtracting product purchases) for all distributors who ever signed up,** including those not now active. If they fail to furnish such data, they are not providing the balanced information you need to make an informed decision.

3. THE GOLDEN RULE TEST

How did you feel about the way you were recruited to do the business, and how do you feel about approaching your family and friends in the same way? **How important are your relationships to you?** Are you offended when they attempt to exploit your connection with them for monetary gain? **Would you want to do the exploiting?**

4. THE TIME FREEDOM TEST

The perennial dream of those with a pyramidal mentality is to be successful at recruiting a downline that will bring in enough money to support them so they won't have to work themselves - thus giving them "time freedom." They can then "leverage" their time by living off the efforts of others.

5. THE SUPPORT TEST

Does the company offer an adequate support infrastructure to handle a temporary burst of volume?

Will your upline be there when you need them, or do they have a history of jumping ship when the next hot MLM deal comes along?

Are conferences and training programs, audio and video tapes, etc., free of charge (as is the case elsewhere for company sponsored programs), **or are you expected to pay for them-as another revenue source for the company?**

Formulated by Jon M Taylor, MD

www.mlm-thetruth.com

CLOSE-UP

On the Street

The public space of streets, neighborhoods and communities is being mapped and targeted by viral marketers and fake grassroots organizations. In some cases the campaigns are overt but, increasingly, street "agents" are making unannounced social approaches.

Product seeders circulate at sports events to find influential young players to wear their gear. Others wander the street wearing colored corporate tattoos. Personal space is the last frontier for commerce. As citizens attempt to retreat from the deluge of advertising they can now be pursued and stalked as soon as they walk out the door.

TACTIC: Neighborhood identities spread the buzz

Viral marketing firm "Alt Terrain" boasts that it has its agents planted throughout the communities of many big cities; the website claims that custom-tailored word-of-mouth and influencer marketing programs (online and offline) spread consumer product buzz to the masses. The "proprietary word-of-mouth networks" include DJs, salon workers, retail shop owners, magazine writers, restaurant staffs, online community leaders, bartenders, magazine photographers, musicians, webmasters and nightclub promoters. The networks are located in New York City, Chicago, San Francisco, Boston, Detroit, Philadelphia, Los Angeles, Portland and Seattle.

www.altterrain.com

Undercover marketing

Undercover marketing is a subset of guerrilla marketing where the consumer doesn't realize they're being marketed to. For example, a marketing company might pay an actor or socially adept person to use a certain product visibly and convincingly in locations where target consumers congregate. While there, the actor will also talk up their product to people they befriend in that location, even handing out samples if it is economically feasible. The actor will often be able to sell consumers on their product without those consumers even noticing it. *Also known as "roach baiting."*

WIKIPEDIA

"It is real-life product placement, there is no product undercover marketing cannot help... You're going to see real people being sponsored by companies. It's not going to be a superstar but Joe Average, and it'll be cheaper, effective and have more credibility."

JONATHAN RESSLER, PIONEER OF UNDERCOVER VIRAL MARKETING

UNDERCOVER Viral Marketing

"It is a form of cultural corruption at a time when advertising already pervades the landscape. It's much more insidious because marketers are creating culture at the grassroots level, on the streets and where we live."

KALLE LASN, EDITOR OF *ADBUSTERS* MAGAZINE

RESOURCE: How to spot the buzz agent

Buzz agents lurk in many different urban environments. One campaign for the Sony-Ericsson T68i phone reveals the disguises of agents that have been deployed...

Leaners - Attractive undercover actors who "lean" over the bar at popular clubs "casually" mentioning a brand name or slogan.

Fake Tourists - Teams of couples posted at popular tourist locations and had passers-by take their pictures with the new phone.

Lost Phones - Replica phones were dropped in high traffic visible locations.

Golf Caddies - Branded Golf Caddies took pictures of foursomes with the T68i as they were waiting to tee off and then emailed the photos from the phones to the customers.

Street Teams - Over 500,000 pieces were passed out by street teams.

Airport Shuttle - Created a Sony Ericsson wrapped luxury shuttle bus that provided free rides to business travelers

TAKE CONTROL

Look out for buzz agents in your local recreational venues. If you think their tactics are ethically questionable, register your concern with the management or local council member.

CASE STUDY: Bombarding the consumer

With a mission to bombard and overwhelm consumers with advertising messages as they go about their daily lives, GoGorilla looks set to succeed. In their view, there is "nothing more regrettable than an empty space with no advertising printed on it." The company web site offers a large selection of original media for viral communication, including stickers for dollar bills, methods for advertising during school camps and instructions on projecting sponsored messages in public spaces.

www.gogorillamedia.com

TACTIC: Computer game campaign targets men

A patron of a local hotspot in San Francisco witnessed a beautiful woman, dressed in black, approaching him and whispering in his ear to "save me." Following this she left behind a business card. Ringing the phone number didn't result in a romantic adventure but instead connected through to an information line about

Electronic Arts' new online computer game "Majestic." The marketing company that designed the campaign reported that 60% of the men approached called the number. Other tactics in the same campaign included staged public "stunts" designed to attract news coverage, and messages scrawled in lipstick on the mirrors of clubs washrooms. The campaign impacted an estimated one million people, resulting in a doubling of sign-ups to the game.

Source: Asiaweek, www.ammomarketing.com

CASE STUDY: Agents mix in public areas

Vespa hired male and female models to hang out on their scooters outside cafés and nightclubs posing as bike gangs. Bypassers were offered promotional items and information if they stopped to admire. Some companies place undercover employees inside record shops and bookstores posing as customers. They are directed to strike up a "spontaneous" conversation about particular items. As yet, there are no ethical or legal guidelines to limit this practice.

Source: Asiaweek

TAKE ⚠ **CONTROL**

Register your opposition to manipulative promotions directly with the brand owners. Advertising regulators are slow to react to new developments in this area. Telephone your complaint directly to the advertiser.

CASE STUDY: Aiming for "Heartshare"

One marketing firm boasts that it goes to extreme lengths to create loyal customers. "Heartshare evolves when brands build an emotional connection with consumers. It's a deep relationship that forms when a brand takes the time to really understand... Ammo infuses brands with human spirit that earns heartshare."

Their approach is bound to be successful as it goes beyond the normal role of information and publicity to get inside your head. Their ground-breaking viral campaigns used such influentials as "entertainment lawyers, celebrity personal assistants, influential non-profit directors" and strategically placed their clients' Volvo cars in highly visible locations.

www.ammomarketing.com

CASE STUDY: Car maker plants trendsetters

Who is behind the wheel of that flashy new car? In one recent example Ford Motor Co. used a group of influential local identities such as DJ's and rock personalities to spread across New York, Miami, Los Angeles, Chicago and San Francisco. They were each given a *Ford Focus* to drive for 6 months. They were given instructions to hand out promotional material to anyone who was interested. The campaign was designed to create a "cool" image for the vehicle.

Source: Business Week

TAKE ⚠ CONTROL

Talk about underground marketing with your friends. Find out where they stand on using relationships for profit, or to promote another company's products.

TREND: Flash mobs

Mobium is an up-and-coming viral marketing firm that claims to have invented the "Flash Mob" phenomenon, where a crowd of people spontaneously take part in unusual pre-organized street theater. They call it *Flash Mobium*, defined as "A large group of people who gather in a usually predetermined location, perform some brief act of integrated business branding, and then quickly disperse... Arranged via web sites and e-mails, flash mobium members voluntarily and simultaneously converge to the venue mentioned in a general e-mail and then collect detailed instructions for the event." Flash mobs have been known to congregate in or near particular shops or business location.

www.mobium.com

TACTIC: Product seeding

Some companies rely on product seeding to gain exposure for new merchandise. In the highly competitive sports shoe market product seeders sometimes descend on sports events in an effort to coax influential players to wear their gear. Using the psychological technique of *social proof* - where people tend to conform to those around them – product seeding campaigns have been very successful in attracting attention and sales in highly competitive youth markets.

Astroturf organizations

Known by some as "democracy for hire," fake grassroots campaigns can sprout up overnight on the whim of an oil company, chemical firm, pharmaceutical manufacturer or tobacco brand. They may look like everyday petitioners or picketers, but they are funded and directed by big corporations.

"Unlike genuine grassroots activism which tends to be money-poor but people-rich, astroturf campaigns are typically people-poor but cash-rich. Funded heavily by corporate largesse, they use sophisticated computer databases, telephone banks and hired organizers to rope less-informed activists into sending letters to their elected officials or engaging in other actions that create the appearance of grassroots support for their client's cause."

> **TAKE !**
> **CONTROL**
> **Look into the organizations who approach you for signature.** Ask them how they are funded and how long they have been operating for before you offer your support.

William Greider's 1992 book, *Who Will Tell the People*, described an astroturf campaign run by Bonner & Associates as a "boiler room" operation with "300 phone lines and a sophisticated computer system, resembling the phone banks employed in election campaigns. Articulate young people sit in little booths every day, dialing around America on a variety of public issues, searching for 'white hat' citizens who can be persuaded to endorse the political objectives of Mobil Oil, Dow Chemical, Citicorp, Ohio Bell, Miller Brewing, US Tobacco, the Chemical Manufacturers Association, the Pharmaceutical Manufacturers Association and dozens of other clients. This kind of political recruiting is expensive but not difficult. ... Imagine Bonner's technique multiplied and elaborated in different ways across hundreds of public issues and you may begin to envision the girth of this industry... This is democracy and it costs a fortune."

www.disinfopedia.org

TACTIC: Personal tattoos

One man sold the "ad space" available on his head to promote a web hosting company. After holding a personal auction, Jim Nelson, 22, of Illinois, has the words "C I Host" and"Managed Web Hosting" tattooed to the back of his head. The tactic has paid off well for the company, who have received hundreds of new customers as a direct result of the tattoo.

"**Brighthouse Institute for Thought Sciences** bridges the gap between business and science and provides its clients with unprecedented insight into their consumers' minds. The company plans to change the marketing world forever by using science to observe and understand the true drivers of consumer behavior. The Thought Sciences team uses functional Magnetic Resonance Imaging (fMRI), a safe and non-invasive technique, to identify patterns of brain activity that reveal how a consumer is actually evaluating a product, object or advertisement."

COMPANY PRESS RELEASE

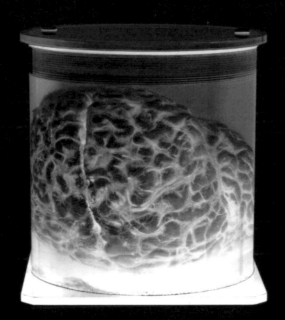

The agreement with Mr. Nelson requires that he display the tattoo for five years and distribute business cards and flyers to those who show interest.

webadvantage.net

TACTIC: Neuromarketing

Corporations are going to new lengths to probe the minds of consumers – literally tapping into their brains. The Brighthouse Institute for Thought Sciences, in Atlanta, is scanning people's brains with MRIs, in an effort to record our subconscious thoughts and devise more seductive advertising.

The process is being called neuromarketing. By mapping these MRI's, they are hoping to determine specific biological triggers that can be used by marketers to attract attention and stimulate purchases. Freud and Jung made significant discoveries about the connection between language and behavior. Brighthouse are hoping to successfully locate, identify and harness these processes.

www.thoughtsciences.com

TAKE !
CONTROL

Visit the web sites of companies such as The Brighthouse Institute and evaluate them for yourself. Note clients who have decided to use the research and marketing strategies which tap into your subconscious.

CLOSE-UP
Children and Families

The deep bonds within a family create trust and confidence. Those connections have now become an effective conduit for corporate branding campaigns.

For many parents who think they can block out mass media advertising, there is still an open channel. Today's children are effective undercover transmitters of advertising, and control an increasing share of the household economy. As family roles change, the power of the child has increased. Advertising impacts parents indirectly, via pre-teen powerbrokers who have mastered the politics of guilt.

TREND: Parents control less of their spending

James McNeal, former marketing professor at a Texas university and now a private consultant, says kids 14 years of age and younger influence a staggering $600-billion in spending every year... "Parents really have ceded household decision-making to kids," he says, arguing that the patriarchal society has been replaced by "filiarchy." Reasons: Guilt, fertility rates, double incomes.

www.workopolis.com

CASE STUDY: The "BrandChild" web site

One research organization is upbeat about the trend they have observed in the control of household decisions. They have authored a major global research study into the influence of children over their parents.

Children in the US spend more than $120 billion of their own money, and influence another $249 million.

tweens aged 9 to 14 don't just influence family purchases such as breakfast cereals, but have a major say on adult purchases such as cars, cell phones and fashion items. Forget the nag factor, our children's research demonstrates that a substantial proportion of parents ask their kids' opinion when making major purchase decisions.

BRANDCHILD.COM

The New Chain of Command

How they use your kids to target your wallet.

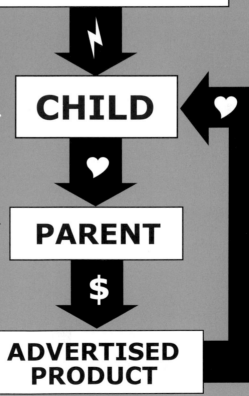

"Kids are the most pure consumers you could have... They tend to interpret your ad literally. They are infinitely open."

Debra McMahon,
Mercer Management Consulting.
Reported in *BusinessWeek*

ADVERTISING

CHILD

PARENT

ADVERTISED PRODUCT

The research discovered that up to one third of this sector has developed an "emotional bond" to specific brands, and that these brands are likely to influence their decisions as adults.

www.brandchild.com

> **TAKE** ⚠ **CONTROL**
> **Spend time with your children as they watch television.** Monitor the way certain foods and toys are promoted and discuss these things with each child.

"Toy Guy" consumer advocate paid by toy manufacturers

Parents who are determined not to listen to their children for advice on which toy to buy have another unexpected obstacle. Consumer advocates who are respected for their objectivity and impartiality may sometimes be compromised.

Christopher Byrne, a consumer advocate known as the Toy Guy, appears on dozens of television and radio shows, especially around Christmas time. What most people don't know is that he is also a paid spokesperson for many manufacturers, which have included Nintendo, Mattel, Fisher-Price, Leapfrog and Hasbro.

OPEN LETTER: The use of psychology to exploit and influence children for commercial purposes

"Commercial Alert and sixty psychologists and psychiatrists sent a letter today to Dr. Richard Suinn, President of the American Psychological Association, urging the Association to restrict the participation of psychologists in advertising or marketing to children. The letter was written by Gary Ruskin, Director of Commercial Alert. The letter follows... We are concerned that members of the APA are ignoring [professional codes of conduct], for monetary gain. They are not using their knowledge to mitigate the causes of human suffering. They are using it instead to promote and assist the commercial exploitation and manipulation of children. As individuals, that is their right, of course. But as a profession dedicated to human welfare, psychologists have a responsibility to the public. The APA should not condone such behavior among its members, nor should psychologists look the other way."

Commercial Alert proposed a "Parents' Bill of Rights" to "help parents combat the commercial influences that prey upon their children and that promote products and values of which parents do not approve."

The nine provisions of the Parents' Bill of Rights are aimed at righting the balance between parents and the **commercial culture and would enable parents to reduce the role of the latter in their childrens' lives if they so choose.**

Parents' Bill Of Rights

Seeks to Restore Parents' Control Over Commercial Influences on Their Children

---

"RIGHT THE BALANCE BETWEEN PARENTS AND CORPORATIONS"

"BAN TELEVISION ADVERTISING AIMED AT CHILDREN UNDER 12 YEARS OF AGE."

" THE RIGHT TO CONTROL ANY COMMERCIAL USE OF PERSONAL INFORMATION CONCERNING THEIR CHILDREN"

"REQUIRES CORPORATIONS TO DISCLOSE WHO CREATED EACH OF THEIR ADVERTISEMENTS, AND WHO DID THE MARKET RESEARCH FOR EACH AD DIRECTED AT CHILDREN UNDER 12 YEARS OF AGE."

"PROHIBITS CORPORATIONS FROM USING THE SCHOOLS AND COMPULSORY SCHOOL LAWS TO BYPASS PARENTS AND PITCH THEIR PRODUCTS TO IMPRESSIONABLE SCHOOLCHILDREN."

"REQUIRES CORPORATIONS TO DISCLOSE, ON PACKAGING AND AT THE OUTSET, ANY AND ALL PRODUCT PLACEMENTS ON TELEVISION AND VIDEOS, AND IN MOVIES, VIDEO GAMES AND BOOKS."

"REQUIRES FAST FOOD RESTAURANT CHAINS TO LABEL CONTENTS OF FOOD"

COMMERCIALALERT.ORG

CLOSE-UP

Cults and Their Tactics

Cults most often attract members through family or friendship links, and their recruiters are usually well-presented, ordinary people. The belief that only gullible or uneducated people fall victim to cults is a widely accepted myth that recruiters exploit with continuing success.

Contrary to popular myth, people who are lured into cults are not mentally deficient or social misfits, (though they may develop such disorders as a result of membership). The average cult recruit is intelligent, well-educated and from a stable family.

Cults demonstrate the most obvious and damaging kind of mind control. There are a range of tell-tale signs that an educational training program or church has crossed the line.

SELF TEST: Are you being recruited?

HYPED MEETINGS

Rather than explain to you what the group believes or what their program is up front, recruiters will instead insist that you can only understand it if you come to a group meeting. There everyone around you will seem so enthusiastic that you will start to think there is something wrong with you. They create an environment where you will feel uncomfortable and the only way to become comfortable is to join them. This is an application of controlled peer pressure.

INTENSE UNRELENTING PRESSURE

They call repeatedly. Meet you on campus or outside your work. Trick you into coming for only an hour and then lead you into a long study, meeting or talk. They have to keep the pressure on, otherwise you might snap out of the mind control environment into which they are trying to immerse you.

THEY TELL YOU THAT THEY ARE NOT A CULT

This is a preemptive strike against the warnings from friends and family members which they know will come. In fact, some cults go so far as to tell you that Satan will try and dissuade you by sending family members and friends to tell you it is a cult. When this tactic is used, a warped form of logic can begin in the recruit's mind: the "agents of Satan" do come and tell them that it is a cult. So since the group predicted that this would happen, the group therefore must be telling the truth! Basically, if any group tells you that they are not a cult, or that some people call them a cult, then find out why!

Adapted from howcultswork.com

> **TAKE ⚠ CONTROL**
>
> **If you are a student, investigate campus organizations independently before joining.** Legitimate religious groups or training providers should be able to suggest references and material for you to evaluate before having to attend a meeting.

Cults recruit 85% via family

85% of people who join a cult do so through a friend or acquaintance. The Premie (Prempal Rawat a.k.a. Maharaji) followers make this their hunting ground. Cult members are charged with getting a friend, colleague or family member to come to a special introductory video screening or to witness a ceremony. (When there, they find everyone must join in.)

TACTIC: The BITE model

Destructive mind control can be understood in terms of four basic components, which form the acronym BITE:

I. Behavior Control – Regulation of lifestyle, habits, time, food, finances

II. Information Control – Use of deception, heavy censorship of internal and external information, spying, propaganda and invasive soliciting of confessions.

Could you fall for this?

" *Those who have that deposit of Life will believe what we say, and know who we are. If they continue in that belief - sustain that Life (though the opposing space alien races will do anything to prevent them from nurturing that gift) they will be protected and 'saved' from the approaching recycling and 'spading under' of the civilization.*"

MARSHALL APPLEWHITE, HEAVEN'S GATE LEADER

If you think you couldn't, you're an ideal cult recruit.

"Look, you don't have to be lazy, crazy or stupid to join a cult. If you are, they don't want you. They want as many rich and talented people as they can sink their hooks into. It's easy to stay out of a cult. Never be tired. Or scared. Too young. Too old. Never get divorced. Or married. Don't strive for success. Don't ever fail. Never hope for world peace. Never feel anger at injustice. Don't be too rich – or too poor. Never experience depression. Never aim for great happiness. Don't get sick. Don't seek – in short, never be vulnerable.

You don't have to be unusual to get sucked in. You just have to be human. I joined my meditation group to clear my mind and improve my grades. Twenty-three years and $150,000 later, I realized my mistake. I screwed up: I wanted something better in life. And someone was happy to sell it to me."

JOHN M. KNAPP, CULT VETERAN, EXECUTIVE DIRECTOR, TRANCENET.ORG

> **WARNING: The documented characteristic known as the Self-Serving Bias is built into each of us. It is a defensive mechanism that produces thoughts like "I'm successful," "it will never happen to me," "only an idiot would fall for that." Cult specialists warn that any normal person is susceptible to the techniques of cults. They warn that even skeptical researchers can be trapped and controlled by basic techniques employed by experienced cult leaders.**

Raëlians
Can 55,000 people all be wrong?

"Rael was contacted by a visitor from another planet, and asked to establish an Embassy to welcome these people back to Earth... The extra-terrestrial was about four feet in height, had long dark hair, almond shaped eyes, olive skin and exuded harmony and humor. He told Rael that... 'Now that you are mature enough to understand this, we would like to enter official contact through an embassy.'" Rael.com

CASE STUDY: Raëlism

Raëlians are a well-resourced and highly organized group employing the trusted formula of "free love" and pseudo-religious UFO myths. They have pulled off a number of major hoaxes, including human cloning claims that have duped major media networks and secured millions of dollars worth of free publicity.

The term Raëlism refers to the belief system promoted by the Raelian Movement, a religious organization which believes that scientifically advanced extraterrestrials known as the Elohim (derived from a Hebrew word appearing in the Torah) created life on Earth through genetic engineering, and that a combination of human cloning and "mind transfer" can ultimately provide immortality. Many people consider the Raëlians a cult.

Claude Vorilhon (born 1946), also known as Raël, founded the Raëlian Movement, which claims to have about 55,000 members from 84 different countries. Membership may be particularly high in France, Japan, Canada (especially Quebec) and the United States (especially Florida). The Movement spreads its message via Raël's books, Raëlian gatherings, and its web site.

The Raëlians promote the social ideas of sexual self-determination and a spirit of sharing and responsibility, which, they claim, will bring a new age of wealth and peace. The philosophy is based on humanitarian values including human rights and freedoms.

Many new members are recruited via attractive female Raëlians who hang out at strip clubs and bars. According to Steve Hassan, former Moonie and cult deprogrammer, "They work the bars and the vulnerable ones are caught... They use free sexuality as inducement and recruiting."
Source: The Edmonton Sun and Wikipedia

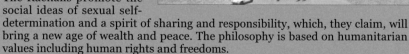

III. Thought Control – Absolute submission to doctrine, loaded language, prolonged thought stopping (meditation, chanting, prayers), enquiry management

IV. Emotional Control – Manipulation of feelings, excessive use of guilt, use of fear, extreme highs and lows, creation of phobias about the outside world.

From Chapter Two of *Releasing the Bonds: Empowering People to Think for Themselves,* © 2000 by Steven Hassan

www.freedomofmind.com

Is it a cult?

If your group has five or more of these characterisics it may be a cult. An estimated 5 to 7 million Americans have been involved in cults, or cult-like groups. The total number of these groups ranges from 3,000 to 5,000. It is hard to get a precise number as cults change their names, splinter off into other groups, or shut down in one area only to open back up in another. There are approximately 180,000 new cult recruits every year.

Exclusivism

The cult projects the idea that their way is the only way. Their group is the only way to enlightenment. It has an US vs. THEM mentality.

Fear and Intimidation

The leader cultivates an atmosphere of fear where no one can question his words. Opposing voices are treated with intensive breaking sessions where they are taught to submit and conform.

Love Bombing

A mind control cult practices love bombing or false love. When you first join the cult you will gain instant friends, you'll be hugged and everyone will want to talk to you. For someone who is lonely or comes from out of town this is especially wonderful. However, after a while this "love" becomes conditional on your performance and/or you measuring up to the cult's unpublished standards.

Information Control

Those who control the information control the person. In a mind control cult any information from outside the cult is considered evil, especially if it is opposing the cult. Members are told not to read it or believe it. Only the cult-supplied information is true.

Reporting Structure

Everyone is encouraged to watch out for "struggling" brothers and report what they see to the leadership. Often information given in deepest confidence will find its way to leadership. Cult members are sometimes shocked to find their problems preached about in the cult meetings. People comment that while in a mind control cult they are acting, always being worried about people watching.

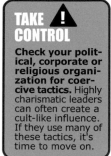

TAKE CONTROL

Check your political, corporate or religious organization for coercive tactics. Highly charismatic leaders can often create a cult-like influence. If they use many of these tactics, it's time to move on.

Loaded Language

The cult will have their own language and terms. These prevent people outside the group being able to engage in "dangerous" conversations with members and it gives the members a sense of belonging. It also allows a phenomenon known as thought-stopping, where a simple word can stop any thoughts in the member's mind which are against the cult.

Time Control

Mind control cults keep their members so busy with meetings and activities that they become too busy and too tired to think about their involvement. Common sense allows us to see that this would be an effective tool for controlling people. The flip side to this is that if a person can get out of the cult's "time control" schedule then after a few weeks, in our experience, they can begin to contrast "normal" life with the controlled cult environment and often this results in them leaving.

Relationship Control

A mind control cult will seek to maneuver your life so as to maximize your contact with cult members and minimize your contact with people outside the group, especially those who oppose your involvement. Cult members will be moved into cult communities or cult housing where they can be watched more closely and immersed in the cult environment. The cult must cut off any contact through which information or reminders of your past life will come. You cannot marry or date anyone outside of the cult and often your spouse will be chosen for you.

Deception

A cult will use deception. The cult will not normally tell people exactly what they believe, their origins, what they practice, and what life is really like in the cult, because if people knew they would not join. This information is taught to the new recruit slowly and in pieces – a "frog in the pot" tactic. Deception is a key pre-requisite to mind control. The cult must be willing to deceive people.

Adapted from: howcultswork.com

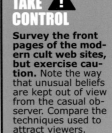

TAKE CONTROL

Survey the front pages of the modern cult web sites, but exercise caution. Note the way that unusual beliefs are kept out of view from the casual observer. Compare the techniques used to attract viewers.

TACTIC: Modern cults use web sites to lure new recruits

Today's cults have penetrated the wealthy, young professional demographic with flashy web sites and online inducements to attract new recruits. The Kabbalah sect that has attracted some high profile celebrities uses a cutting edge multimedia introduction to the "seventy-two names of God" at www.72.com where they also sell *72 names* gear - DVDs and holy Red String. It also targets children through SpiritualityforKids.com.

The Church of Scientology uses an extensive network of websites for their front groups who aim at a range of target markets. Applied Scholastics is the education service, Narcanon is for drug addicts, CBAA.org for businessmen, and BattlefieldEarth.com for youth.

On the following page is a sample of these and other elaborate web sites used by the Moonies, Scientology and other modern cults.

Cults in Cyberspace

www.rael.org	**Raelians**
www.72.com	**Kabbalah Media Initiative**
www.familyfed.org	**Moonies Front Group**
www.scientology.com	**Church of Scientology**
www.dianetics.org	**Scientology Indoctrination**
www.cbaa.org (Businessmen)	**Scientology Front Group**
www.cchr.org (Human Rights)	**Scientology Front Group**
www.battlefieldearth.com	**Scientology Media Initiative**
www.appliedscholastics.org	**Scientology Front Group**
www.krishna.org	**Hare Krishnas**
www.rosicrucian.org	**Rosicrucians**

WARNING: View with care!

These websites are controlled by major cults.
They are used to attract normal, curious people.
Exercise caution when entering.

The Virtual Zone

"People are stunned to hear that
one company has data files
on 185 million Americans."

Ralph Nader

We Know What You Want
Chapter 5: **The Virtual Zone**

Meet your data profile. It makes "choices" for you and shares your personal details, but you can't control it or change it. This electronic identity knows and influences your politics, beliefs, habits and credit rating. It is made possible by the new science of data mining.

Your computer also contains parts of your identity. As we increase our reliance on the Internet our web browsing and purchase habits can be recorded, tracked and distributed, in real time, to marketing firms and government. Automated conversation robots, surveillance technology and hidden computer software monitor your behavior to help others influence your online activities.

In this chapter:

- **Your data profile**
- **Data mining**
- **Hijacking your browser**
- **The new spam**
- **Intelligent agents**
- **Computer games**

CLOSE-UP

Your Virtual Identity

You may not know much about big databases, but they sure know a lot about you. Almost every time you fill out a government form, buy something, visit the hospital or go on holidays your details make their way to one of many major data banks around the country.

Although the data mining industry is in its early years, it has a big future. Information gathering from security cameras, biometrics, implanted devices and public records is increasing in volume and sophistication. This raw data is in turn "mined" at various levels for valuable information. The result is one or more "data profiles," which become a public extension of your life. Because this information determines the precise probability of your response to a piece of voice mail or a magazine ad, it is both powerful and annoying. The profile helps determine which political party will call you, what your life insurance premium will be, whether or not you will be searched at the airport and how much you can borrow. Your data profile leaves a "trail" that allows your shopping habits, health history, religious practices and political activity to be continuously monitored, analyzed and stored.

TREND: Looking for patterns in the data mine

"Data mining is the practice of automatically searching large stores of data for patterns. To do this, data mining uses computational techniques from statistics and pattern recognition.

"Used in the technical context of data warehousing it is neutral. However, it also has a wider, more pejorative usage that implies imposing patterns (and particularly causal relationships) on data where none exist.

"Data mining has been defined as 'The nontrivial extraction of implicit, previously unknown, and potentially useful information from data' and 'The science of extracting useful information from large data sets or databases.'"

−Wikipedia

TAKE **!** **CONTROL**

Make sure the government has your details correct! Monitor your mail. Slight misspelling or a wrong birthdate could result in your being taken for a criminal.

TREND: Merging your profile with others

"Data mining implies scanning the data for any relationships, and then, when one is found, coming up with an interesting explanation. The problem is that large data sets invariably happen to have some exciting relationships peculiar to that data. Therefore any conclusions reached by data mining are likely to be highly suspect. For example, the insurance industry has found that people with good credit records tend to be more likely to make car insurance claims, and have therefore modified their pricing. While this appears to be a legitimate finding, politicians in the United States have queried its legitimacy, on the 'common sense' grounds that how a person handles their credit card doesn't affect how they handle a car. So a finding that is statistically legitimate might not hold up to public scrutiny."

−Wikipedia

TREND: Playing free and easy with your privacy

With governments broadening their definition of terrorism to include activist groups like Greenpeace, you may find yourself under investigation without having committed a crime. Simply belonging to an organization that criticizes the government may be enough to put you under suspicion.

Ebay is one company that has admitted that they will overlook their privacy policy when it comes to the crunch. "If you are under suspicion, your customer details are available." Ebay's Joseph Sullivan said at one conference,

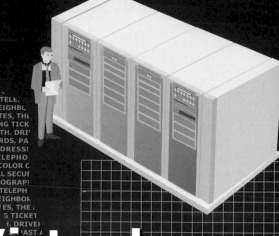

Your Virtual Identity

MEET YOUR DATA PROFILE.

- It exists in a database
- You don't own it
- It can be sold
- You can't change it
- It might have errors

YOUR DATA PROFILE CONTAINS:

> Marriage & Divorce Records
> Past Addresses & Telephone Numbers
> Names & Addresses of Family Members
> Neighbors Addresses & Numbers
> Business Associates
> Registered Vehicles
> Speeding Tickets, Arrests
> Social Security Numbers
> Date of Birth
> Driver's License Photographs
> Spending Habits
> Legal History
> Medical History etc

How your virtual identity "makes decisions" for you.

The highly advanced CAPPS II system used at some airports to assess passengers has led to many dehumanizing incidents for innocent people, but the threat of terrorism remains.

AIRLINE STAFF TYPES YOUR ID NUMBER AT THE CHECK-IN COUNTER

YOUR DATA PROFILE SCANS ITSELF AND RESPONDS with a Green, Yellow or Red assessment.

If the response is Yellow or Red you are regarded as a terrorist threat and search or arrested

Your silent master

Marketing firms and lobby groups use the same method to "quiz" your data profile and decide whether to send you their latest promotion. Your data profile has limited knowledge and unwittingly attracts wasteful junk mail.

Your real "self" has to accept the decision provided by your data profile, which may include humiliating body searches or being barred from your flight.

"If you are a law-enforcement officer, all you have to do is send us a fax with a request for information, and ask about the person behind the seller's identity number, and we will provide you with his name, address, sales history and other details – all without having to produce a court order."

PROFILE: Trusting ChoicePoint with your private stuff

ChoicePoint is probably the largest data mining company in North America. According to its own website, ChoicePoint has amassed 17 billion public records. They include databases from government merged with consumer information, to be combed for marketable lists and profiles. They sell to government departments, employers, insurance companies and direct marketers. Among many data products it lists is CORE Suite – "designed for users who need to draw from a vast number of information resources, including ChoicePoint's 17 billion public records and proprietary data, notes, interviews, photos, financial records and police reports. With CORE Suite, users can quickly and convincingly present investigative findings through compelling diagrams, reports and images."

www.ChoicePoint.com/industry/all_products.html

PROFILE: Deep data digging into your background

DeepIntelligence is a customer profiling service that draws its strength from consumer demographics, business demographics and Yellow Pages databases. You simply provide DeepData with an extract from your customer database of your most profitable customers. DeepData will then match your data against our databases and append valuable information that helps you profile your existing customers.

TAKE CONTROL

Contact your local politicians to register your concern about privacy. Inform them about how much information is circulating on large databases.

www.deepdata.com

RESOURCE: Watching your privacy disappear

Your privacy rights change every day as government security policy evolves and technology advances. This is one website that tracks these changes.

www.privacyrights.org

CASE STUDY: Sifting millions of conversations for consumer trends

BuzzMetrics software system mines millions of online conversations and other commentary to create a database of consumer insight, which is then used by BuzzMetrics analysts to uncover market insight and stakeholder feedback, including measurement of awareness and word-of-mouth levels; qualitative analysis of marketplace perception and attitudes; and anecdotal insight that identifies key market issues, challenges, and opportunities.

"BuzzMetrics monitored a variety of online sources, including doctor and patient discussions, medical journals and media sources, FDA databases, and industry and medical sites to identify key market intelligence. Found numerous pieces of critical strategic insight, including info on competitors' sales tactics, feedback on competitors' unreleased products from clinical trial patients, feedback from doctors and consumers on the client's marketing campaigns, and new market opportunities for the client's products."

www.buzzmetrics.com

PRIZM RESEARCH

"The PRIZM research firm, for example, developed its system of market segmentation in 1974. Using what the demographics industry calls cluster analysis, PRIZM classifies every American neighborhood into forty basic lifestyle segments, or clusters. They then use statistical analysis to look for links between customer characteristics and buying behavior. As PRIZMs promotional material explains, their system offers a definitive battery of consumer data to fine-tune the PRIZM Clusters for behavioral discrimination.

"In processing data from the 1980 U.S. census, PRIZM took every variable in the database (ethnicity, housing, social rank, urbanization) and used computer-generated feedback loops to analyze and compare them to other data recorded elsewhere (new-car sales, magazine subscriptions, real estate transactions and direct-mail responses). From this data, they were able to determine the linkages between a particular demographic cluster and its members likelihoods of buying a car, house, or magazine subscriptionas well as what brands and what types of marketing they were likely to respond to. PRIZM makes it clear that their system explains, predicts, and targets consumer behavior."

– *Coercion*

The Electronic Leash
The future of personal monitoring and control.

Today's defense technology could be tomorrow's ultimate business tool – tracking millions of consumers wherever they are, recording and processing everything they are doing and, eventually, the ability to transmit commands directly to the human brain. It may sound like a corporate fantasy, but these technologies are in the pipeline under obscure names like TIA, Matrix, LifeLog and CAPPS.

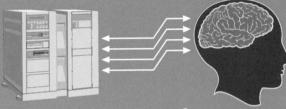

Brain-Machine Interface

DARPA is currently developing a mind-brain machine that will control thought and bodily movements.

Total Information Awareness
DARPA's "Grand Database"

A project known as TIA plans to capture everyone's "information signature" using "revolutionary technology for ultra-large all-source information repositories," which would contain information from multiple sources to create a "virtual, centralized, grand database."

This ominous logo was used briefly for the military's Office of Information Awareness. Major surveillance projects are frequenty renamed using various acronyms and creepy mission statements

LifeLog
A system to record everything a human can feel, see and do.

The Defense Advanced Research Projects Agency oversees major initiatives aimed at monitoring citizens. Its surveillance and data technologies have worried many civil rights activists.

DARPA has commenced the ambitious LifeLog project – a system to monitor every part of a person's life. The future use of this system is not clear , but when combined with other technology, it may end up being the most invasive citizen surveillence apparatus imaginable.

"...sensors capture what the user sees, hears, and feels. GPS, digital compass, and inertial sensors capture the user's orientation and movements. Biomedical sensors capture the user's physical state".

Microchip implants

Some have opted for the convenience of having their personal and medical records surgically implanted in a Verichip®. Small tubes which hold large volumes of personal data, which can be located, retrieved and updated via satellite.

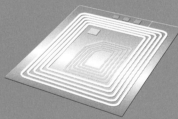

Tiny chips monitor products and customers

Radio Frequency Identification (RFID) tags can monitor individual customers wearing or carrying the tiny antenna chips.

The Electronic Leash
The future of personal monitoring and control.

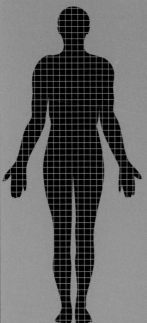

Technologies previously used only in defense, such as security cameras, GPS and biometric systems have eventually found their way into the open market.

Likewise, new surveillance technologies may also prove too tempting for businesses seeking the competitive edge in manipulating consumers. These examples are either in production or under intensive development. The following controversial details have been retrieved from goverment web sites:

#1 LifeLog

STATUS: UNDER DEVELOPMENT

"LifeLog is interested in three major data categories: physical data, transactional data, and context or media data. "Anywhere/anytime" capture of physical data might be provided by hardware worn by the LifeLog user. Visual, aural, and possibly even haptic sensors capture what the user sees, hears and feels. GPS, digital compass and inertial sensors capture the user's orientation and movements. Biomedical sensors capture the user's physical state. LifeLog also captures the user's computer-based interactions and transactions throughout the day from email, calendar, instant messaging, web-based transactions, as well as other common computer applications and stores the data (or, in some cases, pointers to the data) in appropriate formats. Voice transactions can be captured through recording of telephone calls and voice mail, with the called and calling numbers as metadata. FAX and hardcopy written material (such as postal mail) can be scanned. Finally, LifeLog also captures (or at least captures pointers to) the tremendous amounts of context data the user is exposed to every day from diverse media sources, including broadcast television and radio, hardcopy newspapers, magazines, books and other documents, and softcopy electronic books, web sites and database access."

www.darpa.mil/ipto/programs/lifelog/

The Electronic Leash
The future of personal monitoring and control.

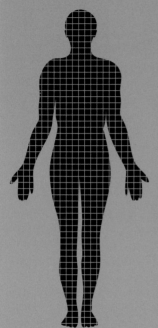

#2 Brain-Machine Interface Program

STATUS: UNDER DEVELOPMENT

A brain-machine interface would be a vital tool for consumer research and potentially an entertainment and advertising medium. "The Brain Machine Interfaces Program represents a major DSO thrust area that will comprise a multidisciplinary, multipronged approach with far reaching impact. [Including] Extraction of neural and force dynamic codes related to patterns of motor or sensory activity required for executing simple to complex motor or sensory activity (e.g., reaching, grasping, manipulating, running, walking, kicking, digging, hearing, seeing, tactile). Accessing sensory activity directly could result in the ability to monitor or transmit communications by the brain (visual, auditory or other). This will require the exploitation of new interfaces and algorithms for providing useful nonlinear transformation, pattern extraction techniques and the ability to test these in appropriate models or systems." - *from announcement Sept 17, 2001 www.darpa.mil*

TAKE ⚠ CONTROL

Investigate new technologies which promise better security. Many new surveillance devices affect the privacy of ordinary people, without a proven increase in safety.

#3 VeriChip Microchip Implants
STATUS: CURRENTLY IN VOLUNTARY USE

Computer chips implanted under the skin are being successfully marketed by Applied Digital Solutions. "VeriChip is an inert, encapsulated microchip that is energized and transmits its information when activated by a VeriChip reader. Because VeriChip is so small (about the size of a pen point) it is virtually undetectable and

The Electronic Leash
The future of personal monitoring and control.

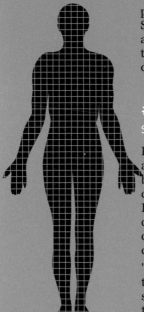

practically indestructible once inserted under your skin. Since the chip has no battery, there are no chemicals to worry about and the chip never "runs down"; its expected life is up to 20 years." The devices can include global positioning devices and personal records. www.4verichip.com

#4 RFID Tags
STATUS: CURRENTLY AVAILABLE

RFID uses radio frequency (RF) identification technology and highly miniaturized computers that enable products to be identified and tracked at any point along the supply chain. While designed to track inventory, Radio Frequency Identification (RFID) tags can also monitor individual customers long after the purchase of the product. One consumer group is warning of "profound implications for consumer privacy." www.stoprfid.com

"RFID chips are now being used on some products, tiny tracking devices the size of a grain of dust, can be used to secretly identify you and the things you're carrying—right through your clothes, wallet, backpack, or purse. Have you already taken one home with you?" www.nocards.org

#5 Matrix Project
STATUS: CURRENTLY DEPLOYED

This database indicates the kind of data being shared by various agencies, providing information on every citizen. It will include credit information, driver's license photographs, marriage and divorce records, past addresses and telephone numbers, names and addresses of family members, neighbors' addresses and telephone numbers, business associates, the make, model and color of registered vehicles, speeding tickets, arrests, social security numbers and dates of birth.

"This system will ensure that state and local law enforcement

The Electronic Leash
The future of personal monitoring and control.

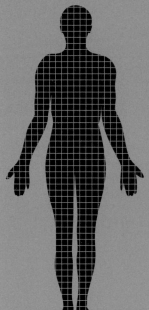

officers – the individuals most likely to come into direct contact with terrorists or other criminals – have the best information (accurate and complete) available to them in a timely manner. It will also provide a mechanism for local officers to share important information they collect 'on the street' with other local, state, and federal authorities. Implementation of this pilot capability represents an important component of an overall prevention strategy, critical to United States homeland security."

www.matrix-at.org

#6 CAPPS II
STATUS: DEPLOYED IN SOME AIRPORTS

The passenger screening system proposed for major airports CAPPS II (Computer Assisted Passenger Prescreening System) shows how your data profile can affect your status as a passenger. Before you board the plane, your passenger data is scanned to determine if your combination of nationality, religion, legal history or personal information makes you a threat to security. You receive a green, yellow or red rating which determines whether you will be subjected to further searches, arrested or allowed to board. Some technology experts note that CAPPS databases may contain out of date data or errors and may result in wrongful arrest, or other embarrassing treatment.

CLOSE-UP

Web Browsers

It's no coincidence that certain online banner ads seem closely matched to your interests at the time. Nor is it by chance that your web browser occasionally acts as though it has a mind of its own, sprouting new accessories or modifying content.

The power of current internet technology, combined with simple programming, enables some companies to track your browser and make invisible modifications to it based on your surfing habits and demographic profile. Your actions can be logged and stored and combined with other data. This information can then be used to decide what information and ads you see on your browser. More invasive applications known as Spyware can be embedded in your computer without your knowledge to record keystrokes and transmit information.

TACTIC: Web sites that hijack your browser

Your browser is probably revealing more than you might want: which computer you are coming from, what software and hardware you are using, details of the link you clicked on and possibly even your email address. For specifics on your browser click on the junkbusters.com demonstration page. Many organizations use "cookies" to track your every move on their site. A cookie is a unique identifier that a web server places on your computer: a serial number for you personally that can be used to retrieve your records from their databases. It's usually a string of random-looking letters long enough to be unique. They are kept in a file called "cookies," "cookies.txt" or "MagicCookie" in your browser directory/folder. They are also known as "persistent cookies," because they may last for years, even if you change ISP or upgrade your browser.

RESOURCE: Junkbusters' web site

Junkbusters is a leading consumer resource on the control of telemarketing calls, unwanted mail, email and commercial invasions of privacy. The company's flagship service, Junkbusters Declare (SM), gives consumers a free and easy way to say what they do and don't want from direct marketers, and to tell companies that sell mailing lists not to "rent" their names. Its other free, web-based service, Junkbusters Spamoff (SM), has become one of the Internet's most popular ways to deter junk emailers. Its widely-used free privacy-enhancing software, the Internet Junkbuster (TM) blocks unwanted cookies and banner ads.

www.junkbusters.com

TREND: Privacy issues with hidden browser agents

TAKE ! **CONTROL**

Test your browser for cookies. Use the cookie analyser at www.Privacy.net to detect which cookies you have and which ones you should remove.

"Cookies also have some important implications with respect to a user's privacy and anonymity on the web. One way is that some companies monitor users' visits to disparate web sites for marketing purposes. Some sites contain images called web bugs (that are transparent and 1 x 1 pixels in size, so that they are not visible) that place cookies on all computers that access them. E-commerce websites can then read those cookies, find out what websites placed them, and send e-mail spam advertisements for products related to those websites."

−Wikipedia

FOCUS: What is Spyware?

Spyware is a special kind of software that is installed along with other applications without your knowledge. Web downloads for companies like Kazaa, Gator and eZula can install, along with the main program, additional programs that affect the behavior of your browser. These unwanted programs can enable external computers to interact with your PC. An updating catalog of spyware creators is at SpywareInfo.com.

The Cray Supercomputer

"The larger question, of course, is whether persuasive technology is a good idea at all, especially when talking about turning a machine as soulless as a computer into what is essentially a propaganda engine."

Denise Roberts, *The New York Times*

"eZula's platform leverages the content that the user is viewing in real time and turns key phrases, that best describe the advertiser, into a global advertising opportunity that drives qualified traffic to the advertiser from anywhere on the web"

ezula.com

Approve   **Cancel**

WARNING: Spyware exposes your computer to other vulnerabilities

Researchers at Spyware Info are warning internet users that spyware can also make your computer more vulnerable to malicious attack. Browser settings... can be forcibly hijacked by malicious web sites and software which modifies your default start and search pages... Sometimes Internet shortcuts will be added to your favorites folder without asking you. The purpose of this is to force you to visit a web site of the hijacker's choice so that they can artificially inflate their web site's traffic for higher advertising revenues... In some cases, these changes are reversible simply by going into Internet options and switching them back. Not always, however. Sometimes it's necessary to edit the Windows registry (gasp!) to undo the changes made. Sometimes there is even a combination of registry setting and files placed on your hard drive that redo your settings every time you reboot the computer."

www.spywareinfo.com

TACTIC: Hiding hijackers in the fine print

TAKE ⚠ CONTROL

Software that promises to improve or change web experience should be researched first. Sites like Spywareinfo.com keep track of risky software.

Kazaa is a highly popular online community with powerful technologies designed to enable interaction and entertainment. Buried in their lengthy "terms of service" (which many people ignore), is a statement that the unused computing power and storage space may be tapped. Their software has been labelled as spyware for embedding extra programs that can be hard to detect. These programs are designed to transmit information about your viewing habits to third party servers.

www.kazaa.com, consumerwebwatch.org

CASE STUDY: eZula converts content to ads in real time

According to their website "eZula's platform leverages the content that the user is viewing in real time and turns key phrases, that best describe the advertiser, into a global advertising opportunity that drives qualified traffic to the advertiser from anywhere on the Web..."

ContextPro™ marks-up, in the form of an underline and a highlight, selected keywords that best describe the advertiser's service or product offerings, on every Web page that contains these keywords across the entire internet. ContextPro™ turns those keywords into active links. Upon a click the user is being linked directly to the relevant page on the advertiser's web site, according to the advertiser specifications.

www.ezula.com

TREND: Tracking and targeting your "needs"

Claria, the maker of Gator, has developed special technology to supply hand picked ads for each separate user. Claria's "behavioral marketing model" is designed to deliver contextually targeted messages. The relevancy of the messages drives click-through and conversion rates up to 40 times higher than traditional banner ads -- boosting campaign results to unprecedented levels. The difference is Claria's deep insights into consumer online behavior. Claria allows advertisers to target consumers based on their individual needs and interests resulting in industry leading ROI, not mass demographically targeted Web site populations.

RESEARCH: The future of online persuasion

Brian Shuster is a pioneer of coercive internet technologies. He has applied for a number of patents that show how desperate web companies are to divert you on your web journey. Amongst his inventions are the pop-up ad or "Traffic Management Utility," an audio ad that can't be switched off, and a hidden web code that diverts your browser to another site without your permission. Here are two of his patent applications...

United States Patent Application 20020022999
Method and apparatus for providing audio advertisements in a computer network

"A method and apparatus for providing audio advertisements in a computer network enables Web sites to deliver audio advertisements that cannot be bypassed by a visitor. More particularly, an advertising or sponsoring Web site receives a request from at least one user for delivery of a user-selected Web page associated with the Web site. The Web site selects at least one audio advertisement from a plurality of audio advertisements for delivery to the user in conjunction with the user-selected Web page. The Web site then delivers the audio advertisement to the user via the network in a format that precludes the user from controlling the manner of playback of the audio advertisement."

United States Patent Application 20020169829
Method, apparatus and system for directing access to content on a computer network

"...system for directing an on-line user to predetermined information. Preferred embodiments of the instant invention interface with the user's browser to utilize the functions of the browser for directing user 'traffic' on a network. In preferred embodiments, when a user accesses a web site page, a traffic control program is executed for the page, wherein the traffic control program controls the transmission (downloading) of data to the user computer and further creates a modified set of rules for at least one of the browser functions. Upon query (or other interaction) by the browser prior to closing page, the traffic control program interacts with the browser software to modify or control one or more of the browser functions, such that the user computer is further directed to a predesignated site or page (and displays a predesignated frame) upon execution of a browser function, instead of accessing the site or page typically associated with the selected browser function. "

TACTIC: Microsoft docs can link to Amazon

By integrating Amazon Web Services, Amazon.com Research Services for Microsoft Office System will provide Microsoft Office System users with convenient and seamless access to Amazon.com from within Microsoft productivity applications via the Research Task Pane. Users will be able to access Amazon.com information and make purchases without launching a browser or leaving their document, e-mail message or presentation. For example, a customer reading a bibliography in a Word document could easily click on a book title and purchase it from within the Research Task Pane without having to leave the Word document. Alternatively, a user will be able to add a footnote, bibliography entry and even cover art for books without needing to manually enter the information into a document.

TREND: Privacy laws overlook the problem

"Privacy legislation that is specific to the Net is probably attacking symptoms rather than the disease," said Junkbusters President and CEO Jason Catlett. He pointed out that Americans still lack the right that most Europeans were guaranteed more than twenty years ago to examine and change the records kept about them by businesses. "People should have a free, simple and legally enforceable way to tell all companies not to sell or 'share' information about them, regardless of whether that personal information goes on the Internet." Junkbusters' written comments before the Federal Trade Commission propose a way that legislators could give consumers the right to protect their names from commercial exploitation without their consent. The proposal extends an existing law governing the US Postal Service, which gives consumers a free way to stop any company from sending them unwanted solicitations by mail, simply by filling out the USPS's brief Form 1500.

BOOK: Persuasive Technology

Can computers change what you think and do? Can they motivate you to stop smoking, persuade you to buy insurance, or convince you to join the Army?

"Yes, they can," says Dr. B.J. Fogg, director of the Persuasive Technology Lab at Stanford University. Fogg has coined the phrase "Captology" (an acronym for computers as persuasive technologies) to capture the domain of research, design and applications of persuasive computers. In this thought-provoking book, based on nine years of research in captology, Dr. Fogg reveals how Web sites, software applications and mobile devices can be used to change people's attitudes and behavior. Technology designers, marketers, researchers, consumers – anyone who wants to leverage or simply understand the persuasive power of interactive technology will appreciate the compelling insights and illuminating examples found inside.

RESOURCE: Consumer WebWatch

Consumer WebWatch keeps track of emerging consumer issues which are unique to the world wide web. It has an archive of research and updates on deceptive tactics.

"The Consumer WebWatch mission is to investigate; inform; and improve the credibility of information published on the World Wide Web... Our goals are to build trust on the Web and provide consumer protection."

www.consumerwebwatch.org

CLOSE-UP
Email and Messaging

Voicemail broadcasting, chat room "bots," and hybrid forms of mass email are the new hidden persuaders. Masquerading as personal contact from a real person, they are actually distributed simultaneously by powerful computers 24 hours a day. Mass-produced word-of-mouth communication is replacing other promotional technologies because of its speed and price. Political campaigners, and other large companies and organizations can produce and deliver these messages with scientifically crafted language to capture maximum response.

TACTIC: Voicemail broadcasting sounds real

Personal phone messages from businesses or political campaigners can turn up in your morning voicemail, having been delivered late at night. Voicemail broadcasters like DialAmerica uses massive computer installations to deliver identical copies of spoken messages to millions of households in the middle of the night. This technique gets around many of the telemarketing obstacles, while achieving a similar objective. One vendor claims that it can fool customers. Their system "plays your pre-recorded message on your customer's answering machine" using "voice mail service, or even to a 'live' person – depending on the voice broadcasting program you choose. The voice on the broadcast message sounds so incredibly real and unscripted, people believe you actually took the time to call them personally!"

www.5star-email-marketing.com

TREND: Sophisticated scripts use language tricks

Lakin Associates advertises a service called Message Engineering™, which includes Neurolinguistic Programming (NLP) scripts to "increase sales and improve the ability to build rapport and influence people on the phone." They boast that their scripts are loaded with "embedded messages," "vocal mirroring" and "predicate mixing," resulting in a massive increase in sales. One case study it cites states that predicate mixing "solves the hang-up problem: if you had an XYZ phone, how do you see yourself deciding to use it... when would you most likely talk to someone?" The mixed use of Visual ('see'), Auditory ('talk'), and Kinesthetic ('use') predicates increased the likelihood that someone would relate to the question and respond."

TAKE CONTROL

Turn the tables on annoying telemarketers.
1. Ask them their full name. If they don't tell you, they may be breaking the law in some states.
2. Get their phone number.
3. Ask them to place you on their do not call list.
If they fail to answer these questions, their company may be subject to a fine.

More at www.ucan.org

TREND: "Word-of-mouse" changes the political landscape

The days of written petitions are coming to a close now that the Internet has enabled rapid cheap communication. These tools enable lobby groups to launch massive action overnight. One of the companies specializing in this area, Mindshare Internet Campaigns, claims several successes in this area including: "100,000 telegrams to the U.S. Congress from a Web campaign with banner ads on leading portals and affinity sites in less than five months for a leading issue group." In 18 days it "Recruited more than 270,000 individuals in an 18-day viral 'word-of-mouse' campaign to oppose a nomination being considered by the U.S. Senate."

TREND: Computerized buddies strike up conversations

Automated agents can imitate real people, carrying on hundreds of simultaneous conversations while subtly promoting their sponsors. These agents drift around the Internet and strike up conversations aimed at promoting products and building brand awareness. Some even coax users by developing in-depth conversations. Patented "Interactive Agent" ActiveBuddy chatted with over 8 million users in one year using instant messenger software.

ActiveBuddy also offers "conversational banners" as an alternative to standard web advertising. *www.activebuddy.com*

"She is so cool and gives really great tips and quizzes about fashion. She also has games you can play on line like hangman, she is awesome even though she is not real she is fun to type to." - ELLEgirl fan

CASE STUDY: Instant "buddy" imitates 16-year-old girl

ELLEgirl used an interactive agent to attract new subscribers. The "ELLEgirlBuddy" offered teens direct and instant access to ELLEgirl.com's teen-savvy news, information, and trends in fashion, entertainment and beauty, as well as the ELLEgirl theme song, through

the ease of instant messaging – a technology embraced by 13 million teens and over 100 million people worldwide. To further engage its users, ELLEgirlBuddy was personality-driven through a custom-developed "voice" for its youthful audience and will complement ELLEgirl with embedded links to ELLEgirl.com. Within the first month, traffic to the ELLEgirl web site increased 83%. Within six weeks, subscriptions to the magazine increased significantly.

Some girls have been taken in by the natural sounding interaction.

FrtnChris: *what are you doing*

ELLEgirlBuddy: *listening to tunes, IMing with my friends, polishing my nails...*

FrtnChris: *I'm bored!*

ELLEgirlBuddy: *well then do something fun!*

FrtnChris: *like what?*

ELLEgirlBuddy: *i dunno... listen to music, go for a walk, learn something new, read a book, be creative! anyway...*

RESOURCE: Junkbusters fight for freedom online

"Junkbusters' mission is to enable you to get rid of any junk mail, telemarketing calls, junk faxes, junk pages, junk email, unwanted banner ads and any other solicitations that you don't want, while still allowing or even encouraging whatever you do want. We provide detailed information on how to stop any company from sending you stuff you don't want."

www.junkbusters.com

CASE STUDY: Instant desktop boyfriend

"Download your desktop boyfriend. *More* magazine has launched a viral campaign in the UK in which it offers readers the chance to download a desktop boyfriend. The only problem is that you have to dump him after two weeks... A short but intense relationship."

www.moremagazine.co.uk

TREND: Spamming is easy

The dark truth about spam is that it actually works. Attempts are being made to make it illegal, but given the global expanse of the Internet, it will keep emerging in some form. Bulk email address collecting programs that can be purchased by anyone roam the web every day, harvesting email addresses from websites and testing them. These email addresses can in turn be purchased by the millions on CD-ROM. 101 Email Address Spider claims that extracting addresses is as easy as using an Internet search engine. Type in the desired keywords and it begins searching the web, extracting email addresses from any page containing those words. With this tool, you can easily and quickly set up your own business mailing lists.

Mind Changing Patents
See special Appendix at back of book

CLOSE-UP

Computer Games

The world computer game market is bigger than the television and movie industries combined and it has had a marked impact on culture and commerce. Unlike television it is self-financing and does not rely on advertising, however, businesses and progressive governments are utilizing it as a tool for influence.

TREND: Computer games with advertising

Computer games are an ideal medium for advertising, given their hypnotic effect on players and the advent of realistic graphics in the latest game consoles. Terry Donovan, Chief Operating Officer of Rockstar Games, was quoted as saying "When you consider the volume of sales, the target demographic, the amount of involvement players have, and the multiple direct and subliminal qualities of branding in that involvement, you have a huge value that has yet to be truly appreciated by advertisers."

CASE STUDY: Jam International – press release

JAM International Partners, Inc., is a company specializing in the product placement of world-renowned brands within the computer and video games industry. Their press release claims the demand is high: "JAM International is the one-stop-shop for in-game product placement, acting as the conduit between the game developer and the brands being placed in the games themselves... Though only open for business a short time, the company's unique services are already in demand. Says Mr. Ross from his New York office, 'The interest in our organization and offerings have far exceeded our expectations. We've been thrilled by the positive response we've received from game developers, publishers and brands looking for product placement opportunities in video games.'"

jaminternational.com

TACTIC: Games a great medium to reach kids

A million dollars seems to have bought a new videogame called "Darkened Skye." The Mars Company enlisted Simon & Schuster Interactive to make a game based on Skittles candy, and the move has reignited the age-old debate over product placement in video games, a practice that has gone on for years. The main argument for using recognizable products is that they lend a realistic flavor to gameplay.

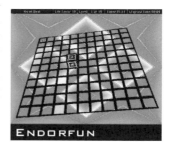

TREND: Subliminal messaging in games

The first computer game to contain intentional subliminal messaging was a puzzle game called "Endorfun." Amongst the flashing colors and upbeat music, messages were flashed on the screen at speeds faster than humans can perceive. The messages were meant to be positive: "I love the world and the world loves me," "It's OK for me to have everything I want." The potential uses of this technology are alarming, particularly if they are included in software without notifying the user.

America's Army

The US Military recently released an action computer game that some felt was a thinly veiled attempt to secure support for the War on Terror. According to a military press release, "*America's Army* was designed and developed so that young Americans could explore Soldiering in the U.S. Army through the virtual portal of online game technology. Through this virtual experience, young Americans can advance through progressive experiences ranging from basic training at Fort Benning, GA, to Special Forces Assessment and Selection at Fort Bragg, NC. Along the way, they can join various elite Army units and experience the power of Army teamwork, values and technology within an engaging format."

AMERICA'S ARMY

Harmless fun? Or is it the new face of propaganda?

*"**America's Army** was designed and developed so that young Americans could explore Soldiering in the U.S. Army through the virtual portal of online game technology."*

GOVERNMENT PRESS RELEASE

WARNING: Some games carry the ultimate risk

A Hong Kong computer game enthusiast was recently found slumped dead at a terminal in a game center after playing non-stop for hours. The 28-year-old was found slumped at his screen early one Saturday after he apparently had been playing the online game "Diablo II" since Friday evening. A similar incident occured in Hong Kong the previous year.

Source: Sydney Morning Herald

US006017302A

United States Patent [19]

Loos

[11]	Patent Number:	**6,017,302**
[45]	Date of Patent:	**Jan. 25, 2000**

[54] **SUBLIMINAL ACOUSTIC MANIPULATION OF NERVOUS SYSTEMS**

[76] Inventor: **Hendricus G. Loos**, 3019 Cresta Wy., Laguna Beach, Calif. 92651

[21] Appl. No.: **08/961,907**

[22] Filed: **Oct. 31, 1997**

[51] Int. Cl.[7] **A61B 5/00**
[52] U.S. Cl. **600/28**
[58] Field of Search 600/26–28; 128/897, 128/898

[56] **References Cited**

U.S. PATENT DOCUMENTS

4,124,022	11/1978	Gross .	
4,335,710	6/1982	Williamson	600/28
4,573,449	3/1986	Warnke .	
5,076,281	12/1991	Gavish	600/28 X
5,123,899	6/1992	Gall	600/28
5,309,411	5/1994	Huang et al.	367/140
5,733,240	3/1998	De Visser	600/9

Primary Examiner—Samuel Gilbert

[57] **ABSTRACT**

In human subjects, sensory resonances can be excited by subliminal atmospheric acoustic pulses that are tuned to the resonance frequency. The ½ Hz sensory resonance affects the autonomic nervous system and may cause relaxation, drowsiness, or sexual excitement, depending on the precise acoustic frequency near ½ Hz used. The effects of the 2.5 Hz resonance include slowing of certain cortical processes, sleepiness, and disorientation. For these effects to occur, the acoustic intensity must lie in a certain deeply subliminal range. Suitable apparatus consists of a portable battery-powered source of weak subaudio acoustic radiation. The method and apparatus can be used by the general public as an aid to relaxation, sleep, or sexual arousal, and clinically for the control and perhaps treatment of insomnia, tremors, epileptic seizures, and anxiety disorders. There is further application as a nonlethal weapon that can be used in law enforcement standoff situations, for causing drowsiness and disorientation in targeted subjects. It is then preferable to use venting acoustic monopoles in the form of a device that inhales and exhales air with subaudio frequency.

17 Claims, 5 Drawing Sheets

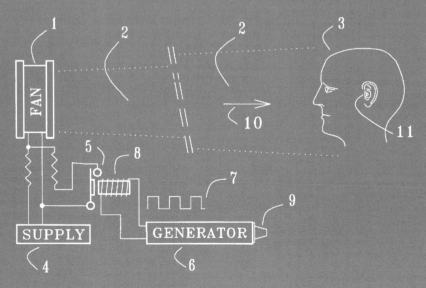

We Know What You Want
Appendix: **Mind-Changing Patents**

Although subliminal advertising remains illegal, there is a race to develop the technology to facilitate it. The US Patent and Trademark Office has a growing number of patents devoted to this endeavor.

Many of the following inventions represent the end-game of human persuasion – regulated subconscious behavioral control by invisible means. With the rapid erosion of basic human rights in the quest for security, combined with the massive corporate push for more invasive influence, these inventors must be increasingly confident that their inventions will eventually be available for use.

Mind Changing Technologies From the Archives of the US Patents Office

Nervous System Manipulation by EM Fields From Monitors

USP # 6,506,148 (January 14, 2003): Loos, Hendricus

Abstract: Physiological effects have been observed in a human subject in response to stimulation of the skin with weak electromagnetic fields that are pulsed with certain frequencies near 1/2 Hz or 2.4 Hz, such as to excite a sensory resonance. Many computer monitors and TV tubes, when displaying pulsed images, emit pulsed electromagnetic fields of sufficient amplitudes to cause such excitation. It is therefore possible to manipulate the nervous system of a subject by pulsing images displayed on a nearby computer monitor or TV set. For the latter, the image pulsing may be imbedded in the program material, or it may be overlaid by modulating a video stream, either as an RF signal or as a video signal. The image displayed on a computer monitor may be pulsed effectively by a simple computer program. For certain monitors, pulsed electromagnetic fields capable of exciting sensory resonances in nearby subjects may be generated even as the displayed images are pulsed with subliminal intensity.

Pulsative Manipulation of Nervous Systems

USP # 6,091,994 (July 18, 2000): Loos, Hendricus

Abstract: Method and apparatus for manipulating the nervous system by imparting subliminal pulsative cooling to the subject's skin at a frequency that is suitable for the excitation of a sensory resonance. At present, two major sensory resonances are known, with frequencies near 1/2 Hz and 2.4 Hz. The 1/2 Hz sensory resonance causes relaxation, sleepiness, ptosis of the eyelids, a tonic smile, a "knot" in the stomach or sexual excitement, depending on the precise frequency used. The 2.4 Hz resonance causes the slowing of certain cortical activities, and is characterized by a large increase of the time needed to silently count backward from 100 to 60, with the eyes closed. The invention can be used by the general public for inducing relaxation, sleep or sexual excitement, and clinically for the control and perhaps a treatment of tremors, seizures and autonomic system disorders such as panic attacks. Embodiments shown are a pulsed fan to impart subliminal cooling pulses to the subject's skin, and a silent device which induces periodically varying flow past the subject's skin, the flow being induced by pulsative rising warm air plumes that are caused by a thin resistive wire which is periodically heated by electric current pulses.

Electric Fringe Field Generator for Manipulating Nervous Systems
USP # 6,081,744 (June 27, 2000): Loos, Hendricus

Abstract: Apparatus and method for manipulating the nervous system of a subject through afferent nerves, modulated by externally applied weak fluctuating electric fields, tuned to certain frequencies such as to excite a resonance in neural circuits. Depending on the frequency chosen, excitation of such resonances causes in a human subject relaxation, sleepiness, sexual excitement or the slowing of certain cortical processes. The electric field used for stimulation of the subject is induced by a pair of field electrodes charged to opposite polarity and placed such that the subject is entirely outside the space between the field electrodes. Such configuration allows for very compact devices where the field electrodes and a battery-powered voltage generator are contained in a small casing, such as a powder box. The stimulation by the weak external electric field relies on frequency modulation of spontaneous spiking patterns of afferent nerves. The method and apparatus can be used by the general public as an aid to relaxation, sleep or arousal, and clinically for the control and perhaps the treatment of tremors and seizures, and disorders of the autonomic nervous system, such as panic attacks.

Subliminal Acoustic Manipulation of Nervous Systems
USP # 6,017,302 (January 25, 2000): Loos, Hendricus

Abstract: In human subjects, sensory resonances can be excited by subliminal atmospheric acoustic pulses that are tuned to the resonance frequency. The 1/2 Hz sensory resonance affects the autonomic nervous system and may cause relaxation, drowsiness, or sexual excitement, depending on the precise acoustic frequency near 1/2 Hz used. The effects of the 2.5 Hz resonance include slowing of certain cortical processes, sleepiness and disorientation. For these effects to occur, the acoustic intensity must lie in a certain deeply subliminal range. Suitable apparatus consists of a portable battery-powered source of weak subaudio acoustic radiation. The method and apparatus can be used by the general public as an aid to relaxation, sleep or sexual arousal, and clinically for the control and perhaps treatment of insomnia, tremors, epileptic seizures, and anxiety disorders. There is further application as a nonlethal weapon that can be used in law enforcement standoff situations, for causing drowsiness and disorientation in targeted subjects. It is then preferable to use venting acoustic monopoles in the form of a device that inhales and exhales air with subaudio frequency.

Magnetic Excitation of Sensory Resonances
USP # 5,935,054 (August 10, 1999): Loos, H.

Abstract: The invention pertains to influencing the nervous system of a subject by a weak externally applied magnetic field with a frequency near 1/2 Hz. In a range of amplitudes, such fields can excite the 1/2 sensory resonance, which is the physiological effect involved in "rocking the baby."

Apparatus for Superimposing Visual Subliminal Instructions on a Video Signal
USP # 5,644,363 (July 1, 1997): Mead, Talbert

Abstract: A subliminal video instructional device comprises circuitry for receiving an underlying video signal and presenting this signal to horizontal and vertical synchronization detection circuits, circuitry for generating a subliminal video message synchronized to the underlying video signal, and circuitry for adding the subliminal video message to the underlying video signal to create a combination video signal.

Method & Apparatus for Remotely Determining Information as to Person's Emotional State
USP # 5,507,291 (April 16, 1996): Stirbl, et al.

Abstract: In a method for remotely determining information relating to a person's emotional state, an waveform energy having a predetermined frequency and a predetermined intensity is generated and wirelessly transmitted towards a remotely located subject. Waveform energy emitted from the subject is detected and automatically analyzed to derive information relating to the individual's emotional state. Physiological or physical parameters of blood pressure, pulse rate, pupil size, respiration rate and perspiration level are measured and compared with reference values to provide information utilizable in evaluating interviewee's responses or possibly criminal intent in security sensitive areas.

Brain Wave Inducing Apparatus
USP # 5,330,414 (July 19, 1994): Yasushi, Mitsuo

Abstract: A random signal generator outputs a random noise signal to a band pass filter which selectively passes frequency components in the frequency range of a desired brain wave from a subject. The output of the band pass filter is supplied to an automatic level controller. The automatic level controller sets the output of band pass filter to a predetermined amplitude. Then, the output of the automatic level controller is fed to a stimulating light generator, which converts the output of the automatic level controller into a light signal for stimulating the subject in order to induce the desired brain wave from the subject. The light signal is then emitted into the subject's eyes.

Method & System for Altering Consciousness
USP # 5,289,438 (February 22, 1994): Gall, James

Abstract: A system for altering the states of human consciousness involves the simultaneous application of multiple stimuli, preferable sounds, having differing frequencies and wave forms. The relationship between the frequencies of the several stimuli is exhibited by the equation g=2.sup.n/4 .multidot.f where: f=frequency of one stimulus; g=frequency of the other stimuli or stimulus; and n=a positive or negative integer which is different for each other stimulus.

Method & Apparatus of Varying the Brain State of a Person by Means of an Audio Signal
USP # 5,135,468 (August 4, 1992): Meissner, Juergen P.

Abstract: A method of varying the brain state of a person includes the steps of supplying the first audio signal to one ear of the person, supplying a second audio signal to the other ear of the person, and substantially continuously varying the frequency of at least one of the first and second audio signals to vary the brain state of the person.

Method of Changing a Person's Behavior
USP # 4,717,343 (January 5, 1988): Densky, Alan B.

Abstract: A method of conditioning a person's unconscious mind in order to effect a desired change in the person's behavior which does not require the services of a trained therapist. Instead the person to be treated views a program of video pictures appearing on a screen. The program as viewed by the person's unconscious mind acts to condition the person's thought patterns in a manner which alters that person's behavior in a positive way.

System for Assessing Verbal Psychobiological Correlates
USP # 4,699,153 (October 13, 1987): Shevrin, Howard, *et al*.

Abstract: A system for assessing psychobiological conditions of a subject utilizes a plurality of words which are selected to be in four categories as critical stimuli. The words are presented by a tachistoscope to the subject in subliminal and supraliminal modes of operation. Subliminal stimulation of the subject is achieved by presenting the selected words for an exposure period of approximately one millisecond. The supraliminal exposure time is approximately thirty milliseconds. Prior to stimulation, the subject is diagnosed in accordance with conventional psychoanalytical techniques to establish the presence and nature of a pathological condition. The words are selected and categorized in four groups: pleasant words, unpleasant words, words related to a diagnosed conscious pathological condition and words related to a diagnosed unconscious pathological condition. The brain wave responses which are evoked by the stimulation are collected via electrodes and analyzed in accordance with a transinformation technique which is based on information signal theory for establishing a probabilistic value which corresponds to the information content of the evoked responses.

Auditory Subliminal Message System & Method
USP # 4,395,600 (July 26, 1983): Lundy, Rene R., *et al*.

Abstract: Ambient audio signals from the customer shopping area within a store are sensed and fed to a signal processing circuit that produces a control signal which varies with variations in the amplitude of the sensed audio signals. A control circuit adjusts the amplitude of an auditory subliminal anti-shoplifting message to increase with increasing amplitudes of sensed audio signals and decrease with decreasing amplitudes of sensed audio signals. This amplitude controlled subliminal message may be mixed with background music and transmitted to the shopping area. To reduce distortion of the subliminal message, its amplitude is controlled to increase at a first rate slower than the rate of increase of the amplitude of ambient audio signals from the area. Also, the amplitude of the subliminal message is controlled to decrease at a second rate faster than the first rate with decreasing ambient audio signal amplitudes to minimize the possibility of the subliminal message becoming supraliminal upon rapid declines in ambient audio signal amplitudes in the area. A masking signal is provided with an amplitude which is also controlled in response to the amplitude of sensed ambient audio signals. This masking signal may be combined with the auditory subliminal message to provide a composite signal fed to, and controlled by, the control circuit.

Multichannel System for & Multifactorial Method of Controlling the Nervous System of a Living Organism
USP # 3,967,616 (July 6, 1976): Ross, Sidney A.

Abstract: A novel method for controlling the nervous system of a living organism for therapeutic and research purposes, among other applications, and an electronic system utilized in, and enabling the practice of, the invented method. Bioelectrical signals generated in specific topological areas of the organism's nervous system, typically areas of the brain, are processed by the invented system so as to produce a sensory stimulus if the system detects the presence or absence, as the case may be, of certain characteristics in the waveform patterns of the bioelectrical signals being monitored. The coincidence of the same or different characteristics in two or more waveform patterns, or the non-coincidence thereof, may be correlated with a certain desired condition of the organism's nervous system; likewise, with respect to the coincidence or non-coincidence of different characteristics of a single waveform pattern. In any event, the sensory stimulus provided by the invented system, typically an audio or visual stimulus, or combination thereof, is fed back to the organism which associates its presence with the goal of achieving the desired condition of its nervous system. Responding to the stimulus, the organism can be trained to control the waveform patterns of the monitored bioelectrical signals and thereby, control its own nervous system. The results of the coincidence function permit results heretofore unobtainable.

Apparatus & Method for Remotely Monitoring & Altering Brain Waves
USP # 3,951,134 (April 20, 1976): Malech, Robert G.

Abstract: Apparatus for and method of sensing brain waves at a position remote from a subject whereby electromagnetic signals of different frequencies are simultaneously transmitted to the brain of the subject in which the signals interfere with one another to yield a waveform which is modulated by the subject's brain waves. The interference waveform which is representative of the brain wave activity is re-transmitted by the brain to a receiver where it is demodulated and amplified. The demodulated waveform is then displayed for visual viewing and routed to a computer for further processing and analysis. The demodulated waveform also can be used to produce a compensating signal which is transmitted back to the brain to effect a desired change in electrical activity therein.

Electronic System for Stimulation of Biological Systems
USP # 3,727,616 (March 17, 1973): Lenskes, H.

Abstract: A receiver totally implanted within a living body is inductively coupled by two associated receiving coils to a physically unattached external transmitter which transmits two signals of different frequencies to the receiver via two associated transmitting coils. One of the signals from the transmitter provides the implanted receiver with precise control or stimulating signals which are demodulated and processed in a signal processor network in the receiver and then used by the body for stimulation of a nerve, for example, while the other signal provides the receiver with a continuous wave power signal which is rectified in the receiver to provide a source of electrical operating power for the receiver circuitry without need for an implanted battery.

Manufacturers or users on-screen graphic display upon power-off of a television receiver

US PAT NO: 5,430,493 ASSIGNEE: Samsung Electronics Co., Ltd., Kyungki, Republic of Korea

Abstract: A message displaying method upon power-off of a television is adapted to delay power-off execution for a few seconds while performing an OSD, in which the OSD message is stored in a microprocessor under the control of a designated program of the microprocessor so that a company can transmit advertising messages to the viewer whenever the users power off their televisions.

Method and apparatus for producing subliminal images

US PAT NO: 5,017,143 TITLE: ASSIGNEE: Popeil Industries, Inc., Beverly Hills, CA

Abstract: A method and apparatus to produce more effective visual subliminal communications. Graphic and/or text images, presented for durations of less than a video frame, at organized rhythmic intervals, the rhythmic intervals intended to affect user receptivity, moods or behavior. Subliminal graphic images having translucent visual values locally dependent on background values in order to maintain desired levels of visual contrast.

Further information and links at www.HowTheyChangeYourMind.com

RESEARCH

SELF HELP

NOTES

SELF HELP

SELF HELP ◎

SELF HELP ◎

SELF HELP

disinformation